MANAGEMENT THOUGHTS

Inspiring thoughts and ideas on Management of Self,
Family, Friends, Employees, Customers, Competition,
Sales & Service, Marketing, Health and
Happiness and Thinking.

A COLLECTION BY

PROMOD BATRA
VIJAY BATRA

::: THINK INC.® New Delhi.

Published by

::: **THINK INC.**®

G-42, Nizamuddin West, New Delhi 110 013
Tel. 4697971, 4634870, Fax 4647980, 4631957, 4697333
E-mail: thinkinc@del3.vsnl.net.in.

ISBN 81-900019-2-2
© Think Inc.®/Promod Batra, 1999

First Published 1991, Reprinted 1992 (three times)
First revised edition 1993, Reprinted 1993 (two times)
Second revised edition 1994, Reprinted 1994 (two times)
Reprinted 1995 (three times)
Third revised edition 1996, Reprinted 1996
Reprinted 1997 (three times), Reprinted 1998 (four times)
Reprinted 1999

Edited by: Susan Brady Maitra

• Illustrations in this book and over 600 more are available for use
in magazines, brochures, books and advertising from the library of
Think Inc., at the above address.
• For more information about Promod Batra and Vijay Batra's
public seminars, private seminars, management books and
successories, please contact: Think Inc.
• This book is available at quantity discounts for
corporate gifts or other bulk purchases.

Distributed by
UBS Publishers' Distributors Ltd.
5 Ansari Road, New Delhi-110 002
• New Delhi Tel. 3273601, 3274846, 3266647, Fax 3276593
• Bombay Tel. 2046971, 2047700, Fax 2040827
• Bangalore Tel. 2263901-043, Fax 2263904
• Calcutta Tel. 2441821, 2442910, 2449473, Fax 2450027
• Madras Tel. 8276355, Fax 8270189
• Patna Tel. 652856, 653973, 656170, Fax 656169
• Pune Tel. 349491

Designed and produced by
GOODWORD PRESS
1 Nizamuddin West Market, New Delhi 110 013
Tel. 4626666, 4625454, Fax 91-11-4697333

Dedicated to
Mr. H.P. Nanda

—A GREAT MAN
WHO DOES GREAT THINGS
GREATLY.

Selected books by
Promod Batra
and Vijay Batra

- Management Thoughts
- Management Ideas in Action
- Management Think Tank

- Management Thoughts for the Family
- Simple Ways to Manage Stress
- Simple Ways to Become A Professional Secretary

- Simple Ways to Bring Out The Best In Your Employees
- Simple Ways to Make Your Family Happy
- Simple Ways to Generate a Positive Attitude
  Toward Women at the Workplace

- Pearls of Wisdom for the Family
- Pearls of Wisdom for Managers
- Selling Is A Noble Profession

See our complete catalogue at the end of the book.

IN PRAISE OF SIMPLE WISDOM...

In corporate circles he's known as the new age guru of management hometruths. Till recently a senior manager at Escorts, Promod Batra has now opted to devote his life to enlightening executives with his books, kits and other management tools like 'Think Cards', 'Thought Kits' and 'Management Pin-Ups.'

—*The Hindustan Times, 27.8.1997*

Ever heard of an **Anger Prevention Kit?** No? Sentinel came across this kit at PGI. It was displayed in the office of the Registrar, Mr. O.P. Sharda. The kit is simple: It is intended to manage people imaginatively. All it says is "Think: a matchstick has a head, but it does not have a brain. Therefore, whenever there is a little friction, it flares up immediately." Is there a lesson to be learnt? Read on: "You and we have heads and brains. Therefore, let us not react on impulse." "Always... smile."

—*The.Tribune, July 6, 1995*

My Best Reads - P. Chidambaram
Former minister of state for commerce
Management Ideas in Action, by Promod Batra and Deepak Mahendru
"An interesting read."

—*Business Today , May 22-June 6, 1993*

Management Thoughts is Batra's Bible for the big boys of business. Interspersed with witty illustrations, the pages conceal many a surprise. The oft-heard, familiar dictums could well have been drab reproductions from memory. It is to Batra's credit that, more often than not, he skirts the pitfalls. Above all, by virtue of its format the book is racy...

—*Economic Times, March 28, 1992*

Simple Ways to Manage Stress
The 18th century was the age of reason, the 19th of progress, and the 20th of anxiety and tension. Suspicious and distrustful attitudes cause confusion resulting in fear and anxiety. From anxiety comes tension Tension creates stress. Batra in his well got-up book has driven the point in lucid, simple and understandable English with suitable illustrations. **Simple Ways to Manage Stress** is divided into 33 chapters. Starting with "Do it now—Problem solving" Batra explains the MISER concept (merge, improve, simplify, eliminate, reduce) and simple pleasures and foolish pleasures well....

—*The Hindu, August 5, 1997*

Much has been written about what it takes to make a happy famly. It is like casting pearls of wisdom before swine. I can count happy families I know on half the fingers of one hand; unhappy families by the score. Also, happy families tend to be self-centred, unwelcoming towards outsiders and uniformly boring.... . So why all this concentration on a happy family life? I would not pronounce on the subject except for receiving a handsomely produced little booklet **Pearls of Wisdom for the Family** compiled by Promod Batra and Rakshanda Jalil. It is illustrated by my dear friend the late Mickey Patel... .

— *Khushwant Singh, Hindustan Times, April 20, 1996*

Management Thoughts is a delightful compilation of aphorisms, sayings, quotable quotes and insightful nuggets relevant to the practice of the art of business management...

—*BusinessWorld, 4-17 December 1991*

The Bestsellers
Management Ideas in Action, by Promod Batra and Deepak Mahendru, Think Inc. Rs. 266

—*Business Today, April 7, 1993*

Management Thoughts has pointers for situations in which your own attitudinal drawbacks can make the difference between success and failure.

—*Financial Express, October 27, 1991*

Capital Life
Don't lose your head like a matchstick..
If you are given to bouts of temper, all you need, perhaps, is a matchstick. It is, in fact, the main item of an "anger controlling kit" on sale... Promod Batra is a professional manager. He has developed 15 such pocketable kits which put across succinct messages... Apart from these kits, Mr. Batra has 11 Management Books... Interestingly, his books do not have those hardcore management thoughts. They are basically a collection of sayings and thoughts with suitable illustrations... His works include **Management Thoughts, Management Ideas in Action, Management Thoughts for the Family in Business, Management Think Tank.** What relevance do these books have in creative management writing? "These form a part of a manager's personality. He cannot be compartmentalised. Moreover, he will be able to give his best only if he is having a peaceful family life."

—*Delhi Times, September 8, 1995*

New Releases
Pearls of Wisdom for the Family, by Promod Batra
(Think Inc. Rs. 96 each)
A series of cute books full of correct thoughts on the family and happy
living. Classily produced.

—*India Today, August 4, 1997*

At the Book Fair
In the same section, there are some half a dozen interesting titles by Promod Batra who claims to write not from ivory tower but the heart. He shares
gurumantras on how to make your daughter worldly-wise and your son
good for everything, how to keep your wife happy and how to live peacefully with your in-laws... .

—*Tribune, September, 22, 1996*

I am delighted to read in the latest issue of *Business India*, p. 115, 'My Best
Reads' column by former Minister for Commerce, Mr. P. Chidambaram.
He has referred to the book **Management Ideas in Action** authored by you
and Deepak Mahendru.
It is a great compliment. We are proud of you.

—*H.P. Nanda, May 28, 1993*

My Twenty-five Years with Escorts contains advice on every aspect of management. Often these tips and suggestions are expressed in the form of
maxims or pithy sayings or anecdotes which are likely to remain embed-
ded in the reader's memory. To ensure better retention of the author's ideas,
the book is profusely illustrated with cute and attractive, cartoon-like draw-
ings.

—*TA Mathias, XLRI Journal, Jamshedpur, June 1989*

...He deserves thanks for having chosen to share his suggestions, tips and
experiences with the readers. Although **My Twenty-five Years with Escorts**
may not qualify to be a reference book in Personnel Management, it can
claim to be a practical guide.

—*The Hindu, January 17, 1989*

He sold vehicles during his 33-year stint as chief general manager of Escorts Ltd. Today, after retirement, he markets books on management that
he writes. Selling has been Promod Batra's byword, ever since he got an
MBA from Minnesota University way back in the 60s.

Over the years, Batra has collected ideas on management—professional
and personal—and put them together in the form of 20 books. "Management is an art," he says. "My belief is that if you can manage yourself well,

you can manage others better," adds Batra, who was in Bangalore recently to promote his books.

"Life is simple, but you can live it complicated," he says, explaining the tone of his books. So his books, calendars, posters and think cards convey simple, yet significant messages. The next time you want to give a gift to your friend, try Batra's management cards...

Delhi-based Batra has also floated Think Inc., a management firm. Batra explains enthusiastically: "Think is the motto of International Business Machines. We have to think beyond the boundaries. All of us think. Why not think positively and make it help us? We should be able to extract happiness from life."

"Success is a journey, not a destination," he says, speaking about the good response that his books have received. For instance, **Management Thoughts** has sold 15,000 copies in English and 8,000 copies in Japanese, **Simple Ways to Manage Stress** has sold over 5,000 copies in Singapore and Malaysia.

—The Times of India, Bangalore, 30 May 1997

An impeccable dress code, a crisp voice, and an easy, unassuming, confident demeanour. The gentleman on the podium has the gathering enraptured by his wit and erudition. His effervescent personality and exuberance are infectious. He radiates a sense of well being and goodness, which is all-pervasive. His peaceful countenance, pristine innocence and a cheerful childlike smile is akin to that of a yogi, who dwells in an eternal state of nirvana. He is a swell sexagenarian.

Hello Ahmedabad, meet Promod Batra.... According to him thinking is the most important job in management, whether it's management of oneself, one's family, one's employees or one's customers. Says Promod: "In thinking, what matters most is your attitude. The mind can think positively or it can think negatively. If you have to deal effectively with a problem, an opportunity, a note, a report, you ought to be in a positive mood. Only you — and no one else — can put yourself in a positive mood. Wealth, wisdom, position, status (or lack of it) makes no difference. You are your best friend, or your worst enemy."

Promod strongly believes that India could be a global giant. If only we got rid of our muddled thinking and streamlined our thought processes....

—Iqbal Anand, The Times of India, November 19, 1997

With excellent cartoons and supporting text the author takes the reader through a multitude of thought provoking concepts and ideas related to one's personal life and workplace. **Brainstorming for Creativity and Innovation** is indeed an excellent compendium of the "right seeds"...

—BMA Review, January 1997

CONTENTS

ILLUSTRATIONS

INSPIRATION FROM
LORD GANESHJEE

Lord Ganeshjee's **Big Head** inspires us to think big and think profitably; the **Big Ears** prompt us to listen patiently to new ideas and suggestions; the **Narrow Eyes** point to deep concentration needed to finish tasks in hand well and quickly; the **Long Nose** tells us to poke around inquisitively to learn more and the **Small Mouth** reminds us to speak less and listen more.

FOREWORD

The attitude of a person measures the altitude of his success. The world is viewed differently by everyone, and it is an individual's perception that governs his ambition and the way he views the opportunities in this world.

Success, and by implication happiness, is not determined by how much you earn or your station in life. Success is determined by whether or not you achieve your chosen goals in life — whatever they might be. Each person's goals are different, and may even change during the course of his or her life.

What turns goals and dreams, and even limited objectives, into reality — success — are the attitudes one brings to the work of living and doing. If you have an attitude that is appropriate to your objective, success is assured. You cannot fear blood and be a good doctor, or dislike people and be an effective manager. You cannot be small-minded and expect to achieve big things.

It is essential for every individual to crystallise his vision in order to develop his own paradigm and path to success. Once you are clear on what you want to do with your life, your success will depend on how well you cultivate, improve or change the attitudes needed to keep you on target.

This is an ongoing exercise throughout life. One must regularly reflect on one's attitudes and activity, assess them from the standpoint of the goal, and make changes where necessary. It is in this connection that I heartily recommend *Management Thoughts* to you. It contains more than a thousand inspiring thoughts and commonsensical ideas on managing all aspects of life and work, in a very accessible format.

Management Thoughts will help you develop the habit of reflection in a highly enjoyable way.

Nikhil Nanda
March 18, 1996

11

PREFACE

---◆---

Management Thoughts has been a great success. We feel happy and very satisfied and very thankful to our friendly readers who made this success possible.

"In the sky there is no distinction of east and west; people create the distinctions out of their minds, and then believe them to be true."— Anonymous.

It is our pursuit through this as well as our forthcoming publications to address the cultural differences that have been created over the years of human civilisation, and find ways to integrate various styles of business and living practiced in different parts of the world.

It took many years to compile and dare to self-publish the first edition. We are confident that with one of us contributing from across the seven seas, with experience and exposure in American, Indian and Japanese business environments, the future editions are likely to become better and still better.

Thanking you again, our friendly readers. . .

Promod Batra
Vijay Batra

March 3, 1996

PREFACE TO FIRST EDITION

'Think' — I learnt during my M.B.A. years at the University of Minnesota — was IBM's invention. I liked the word very much and, when I started my career at Escorts in 1963, I began using it with 'There must be a better way!' Colleagues, friends, dealers and vendors started showing their appreciation. Then I added 'Do it now!,' 'Ask for it!,' and so on. Soon I started a collection of such expressions; the encouraging response I received prompted me to print and circulate, and later on to publish it.

I have been enlarging my collection during this quarter of a century. And here it is: more than 1350 aphorisms from many, many sources — most of them duly improved and changed to serve the purpose of a Think Tank! In the roles of manager, father, husband and friend, I am greatly assisted when appropriate sayings from this collection flash on my mental screen. I then feel happy and satisfied.

I owe an apology to the authors for not naming them! To me, a good thought is a good thought, whether Lincoln or Shakespeare or Gandhi expressed it! To me each thought is the outcome of many, many minds. For example, the memorable expression "government of the people, by the people, for the people..." is attributed to Abraham Lincoln, but before that Theodore Parker said it, before that Webster, before that James Monroe, before that Wyclif, and even before him Cleon and maybe many more!

To me a thought and its phraseology are what matter most. They inspire me, as I hope they will inspire you.

Promod Batra

July 19, 1991

1
Managing Yourself

Self-knowledge is the beginning
of self-improvement.

1
Think... there must be a better way!

2
Do it now.

3
Ask for it.

4
The future is NOW.

5
Stick your neck out.

6
Keep your mind six to nine per cent empty!

7
A positive attitude pays.

8
Thinking is hard work.

9
Problems are only solutions in disguise.

10
Most problems are really the absence of ideas.

11
Learn by listening. Understand by reflecting.

12
Be daring in setting priorities.

13
Simplify your life!

Stress, in simple terms, is like a fire — more precisely, embers, pe. manent embers. We can either control them to be harmless embers and enjoy their glow, or fan them into huge fires. Not knowing better, many of us do the latter.

14

There is no right way to do something wrong.

15

Making excuses does not hurt anybody but yourself.

16

A liar is not believed when he speaks the truth.

17

A man's reach should exceed his grasp.

18

Strong convictions precede great actions.

19

Think, decide, do what you think is right.

20

The key to success is knowing yourself.

21

Every stone can be a stepping stone.

22

Arrogance is the quicksand of success.

23

The greatest loss is the loss of self-confidence.

24

Learn to say "No"!

25

The bow that bends too strictly snaps itself.

26

Success has made failures of many men.

YOU RARELY SUCCEED AT ANYTHING

UNLESS YOU HAVE FUN DOING IT.

27

I ruined time; now time is ruining me.

28

Experience is one thing you can't get for nothing.

29

The ability to speak is a shortcut to distinction.

30

If you can't stand the heat, get out of the kitchen.

31

Practice makes perfect.

32

Reading without thinking is like eating
without digesting.

33

Ideas, like time and tide, wait for no one.

34

Our trouble is not ignorance, but inaction.

35

When you're sure it's good enough. . . improve it.

36

If you are through learning, you are through!

37

Organise yourself well to have more time
to do the things you love to do.

38

Attitudes are mirrors of the mind;
they reflect thinking.

Even a fish wouldn't get into trouble if he'd keep his mouth shut!

39

Those who cannot remember
the past are condemned to repeat it.

40

Character is the foundation stone upon which
one must build to win respect.

41

You cannot be anything if you want to be everything.

42

If at first you do succeed,
try to hide your astonishment!

43

Don't start something which you cannot stop.

44

Of all the things you wear,
your expression is the most important.

45

There's plenty of room at the top,
but there's ro room to sit down.

46

If you want to gather honey,
don't kick over the beehive.

47

It is sometimes easier to fight for one's principles
than to live up to them.

48

One of these days is none of these days;
today is the day to start the big job.

IDENTIFY YOUR WEAK LINK

...AND ACT NOW!

One weak link can spell disaster for the whole chain. Hence, analyse yourself. See if you have any flaws and frailties that can play havoc with your organisation and your aims.

If you do have an Achilles heel somewhere, attend to it. Remove the weakness. And stride ahead from strength to strength.

49

Admitting you're wrong is a modest way of showing
you've grown a little wiser.

50

Ships are safer in the harbour,
but they are not meant for that purpose.

51

The most important thing for a young man is to
establish reputation and character.

52

Some people pay so much attention to their reputation
that they lose their character.

53

When confessed, the sin becomes less since it
becomes the truth.

54

When the wise get angry, they lose their wisdom.

55

Do not wait for the best idea. Implement the better
idea; still better and the best will follow.

56

Be a lion at heart and
do not forget the tact of a fox.

57

By working sincerely for eight hours a day,
you can get promoted to be a boss and
work twelve hours a day.

Empty your mind!

The average man empties his pockets onto his dresser or desk before retiring. Personally, I rather enjoy standing over a wastebasket during this process to see how many things I can throw away: notes, memos, scraps of paper, completed self-directions, even knick-knacks which I have picked up.

It is perhaps even more important to empty the mind in this way. During the day we pick up mental odds and ends: a little worry, a little resentment, a few annoyances, some irritations, perhaps even some guilt reactions. Every night, these should be thrown out. Unless discarded, they accumulate and are bound to prevent clear thinking.

© Think Inc./Promod Batra

58

Even if you're on the right track, you'll
get run over if you just sit there.

59

At the start of your career, what you learn is more
important than what you earn.

60

If you do not know how to speak,
better learn how to keep quiet.

61

The people who make haste are usually saving
minutes after having wasted hours.

62

There is no indigestion worse than that which comes
from having to eat your own words.

63

Take the decision. If it is right, well and good.
And if it is wrong, you will find out soon enough.

64

Leadership usually gravitates to the man
who can get up and say what he thinks.

65

There is no expedient to which a man will not
resort to avoid the labour of thinking.

66

The average man develops only ten per cent of
his latent mental ability.

Kites rise against, not with the wind.

Like they say, "The gem cannot be polished without friction, nor the man without trials." Look adversity directly in the eye and it will diminish in size. Face it with conviction because only if you go through the wars bravely, will you get the medals. And, isn't it always more fun to win a hard fight than an easy one?

67

You will have no quarrels with life, as long as
you have something to do when
you get up every morning.

68

One can see the heavens
through a needle's eye.

69

It is not enough for a man to know how to ride;
he must know how to fall.

70

Ninety per cent of the decisions can be taken
immediately on the basis of past experience
and only ten per cent require in-depth analysis.

71

Crossing your bridges when you come to them
and exploiting opportunities when they
come your way are the real secrets
of success in this world.

72

A vacation should be just long enough for the boss to
miss you, and not long enough for him to discover
how well he can get along without you.

73

When we are not engaged in thinking about some
definite problem, we usually spend about 95 per cent
of our time thinking about ourselves.

74

Treat every problem as a roadblock which forces
you to take a detour. You may find the best during
this forced detour, if your mind is active and vigilant.

75

If you have a rupee and I have another,
And we exchange, we have one rupee each;
If you have a better idea and I have another,
And we exchange, we have two better ideas each.

76

Any fool can criticise, condemn and complain—
and most fools do.

77

The fire you kindle for your enemy burns
yourself more than him.

78

Stop existing. Start living.

79

Honesty is still the best policy, with a
little bit of common sense.

80

There is always one thing more to do.

81

Be willing to spend today for tomorrow's growth.

82

Education is the ability to meet life's situations.

...BEST WAY
TO
MAKE YOUR DREAMS
COME TRUE IS TO
WAKE UP...

83

The great aim of education is not knowledge
but action.

84

It's what you learn after you know it all that counts.

85

It is foolish to learn things that one has to
forget later on.

86

Either I will find a way or make one.

87

A man can succeed at almost anything for which
he has unlimited enthusiasm.

88

In his first year in the automobile business,
Henry Ford went bankrupt.
Two years later, his second company also failed.
His third corporation has done rather well, however!

89

If it were not for the rock in its bed,
the stream would have no song.

90

A manager succeeds or fails not so much
because of what he does, but because of what he is
able to get someone else to do.

91

Unless you are forced to use your mind, you become
mentally lazy and will never fulfil your potential.

A MAN'S BEST FRIEND IS A DOG — HE DOESN'T
DISTINGUISH BETWEEN A RICH OR POOR MASTER!
IT TAKES SO LITTLE TO PLEASE HIM, SATISFY HIM!
...PERHAPS THERE'S A LESSON TO BE
LEARNT FROM 'A DOG'S LIFE'!

92

Napoleon was an early riser. An hour's less sleep
per day will add five years to your working life.

93

Men may blush to hear what they
were not ashamed to do.

94

There is no one way by which you, when you take a
decision, can please everyone.

95

Speak your truth quietly and clearly,
and listen to others, even the dull and ignorant;
they too have their story.

96

Take calculated risks. Doing so is
quite different from being rash.

97

The world's largest fires can be extinguished with a
cup of water at the right time.

98

Learn to live with your mental doors unlocked
so that ideas can get in.

99

A person doesn't learn to choose a good
alternative without choosing a few bad ones.

100

Nothing is impossible for the man who doesn't
have to do it himself.

Do what you think is right and know that it was right.

What will the auditors say? What will my colleagues say? What will my neighbours say? These are immobilising thoughts. Remember the story of the father, son and donkey going to the market. They got so influenced by what people thought of them that neither could ride the donkey. Well, do what you think is right, what you think is proper. As long as it is not in your selfish interest only, go ahead and do it. Remember, you can always rectify wrong decisions the moment you find them to be wrong. But if you do not take any decisions at all, how will you ever be able to improve your future decision making?

101

It doesn't matter whether you can be proud of your
ancestors; what matters is if they can be proud of you.

102

The more noise a man or a motor makes,
the less power there is available.

103

Man has a hidden treasure within.
Difficulties and setbacks bring it forth.

104

There are two ways of spreading light: to be the
candle or the mirror that reflects it.

105

Failure means delay, not defeat.

106

Never show your teeth unless you can bite.

107

The person who can smile when the natural
impulse is to cry wins the admiration and
respect of co-workers and friends.

108

"I cannot do it" never accomplished anything yet.

109

Always tell yourself: The difference between running a
business and ruining a business is "I."

110

Accepting responsibility is accepting challenge.

Every job is a self-portrait of the person who did it.

Autograph your work with excellence.

111

If you want to be a success,
display enough courage to welcome failures.

112

Giving a drink of water to an enemy is like
putting a lump of burning charcoal on his head.

113

God grant me the serenity to accept the things
I cannot change, the courage to change the things I
can and the wisdom to know the difference.

114

All confidence is acquired or self-developed through
positive thinking, which is triggered off by good
books, good friends and good visits.

115

Do not wait for extraordinary circumstances to do
good actions; try to use ordinary situations.

116

There is no blindness
except blindness of the heart.

117

A wise man is one who forgets the faults
of others, but always remembers his own.

118

Big achievements can be made only by a man
who is content with small beginnings.

119

Build your self-respec: via the joy of role excellence.

120

The genuine beauty of acquiring knowledge is that
you can learn anytime.

121

Say "sorry" at the right moment.

122

Chasing after the impossible you lose what is possible.

123

Cut your social functions where your substitute will be
equally good and no one will miss you.

124

The fullest and best ears of corn
hang toward the ground.

125

Like trees, we must each find a place
to grow and branch out.

126

Those who fret over small issues only demonstrate
their inability to find anything big in their lives.

127

Crowding one's life does not always enrich it.

128

Concentration is the secret of strength in war and in
trade; in short, in the management of human affairs.

Do your SWOT analysis today!

Concentrate on your
STRENGTHS

Recognise your
WEAKNESSES

Evaluate your
OPPORTUNITIES

Research your
THREATS

SWOT is a good tool for a manager, like a thermometer and a stethoscope for a doctor! You need an objective mind and a genuine friend to help you do your SWOT analysis quarterly.

Strengths enable you to put your best foot forward. **Weaknesses**? Who does not have them? Only when you recognise them can you do something to correct them. **Opportunities** are aplenty— even in adversity. Only, one has to evaluate them for what they are. **Threats** are like ticking time bombs; defuse them by anticipating and taking preventive action.

129

You do not need to invent the wheel.
Start from where others left off.

130

Glory is a poison that can
only be taken in small doses.

131

Challenge is a part of life—take it in stride knowing
that you will win most of the time, lose some of
the time, but become a better man either
way for having tried.

132

Being honest is like being pregnant: there's no such
thing as a little bit; either you are or you are not.

133

It is difficult to soar with eagles when
you work with turkeys.

134

One pound of learning requires ten pounds
of common sense to apply it.

135

Polished copper is cheaper but makes a
better impression than crude gold.

136

Do the thing you fear, and fear will disappear.

137

All men make mistakes; only fools repeat them.

Manage your time as you manage your money.

Do you know how a 70-year life is generally spent? On an average, 25 years in sleep, 8 years in study and education, 6 years in rest and illness, 7 years in holidays and recreation, 5 in commuting, 4 years in eating and 3 years in transition, i.e. getting ready to do all the above activities.

That leaves only 12 years for effective work. Charles Schwab, an American millionaire, paid a consultant 25,000 dollars in 1936 to advise him how to best use this precious, irretrievable resource. His advice: "Start your day with a 'To Do' list and prioritise the vital few after picking them from the trivial many."

138

Indecision is expensive, very expensive.

139

Learn from failures; do not brood over them.

140

Empty sacks will never stand upright.

141

He who hesitates is lost.

142

A wise man speaks when others have
exhausted their words.

143

Get a good "radar," and keep it sweeping.

144

An open mind collects
more riches than an open purse.

145

You have to be very clever to do simple things!

146

Life is the art of drawing sufficient conclusions
from insufficient premises.

147

If at first you don't succeed, try once more—
and then try something else.

148

One is not born a genius; one becomes a genius.

ALL
ELSE
FAILS...

LOWER
YOUR
STANDARDS

44

149

It is not only machinery that becomes obsolete.
One has to guard against obsolescence of the mind.

150

If you are still tender enough to feel ashamed, thank
God and ask Him to keep you that way.

151

Do not postpone the unpleasant and difficult tasks.
Do them now, and you will feel
much better afterwards.

152

If you make up your mind to do three things,
namely to work, to save and to learn,
you can rise in this world.

153

Influence is like a savings account. The less
you use it, the more you've got it.

154

Keep on learning—from your successes, so you repeat
them; from your failures, so you never
make the same one twice.

155

Keep on mulling your ideas, remembering that even
the best can be made better.

156

Keep on reviewing your basics.

157

To act right, you have to look right and feel right.

Act as though it were impossible to fail.

☐ Think Inc./Promod Batra

158

Life's greatest thrill is tomorrow.

159

Machines must work. Men must think.

160

Many a live wire would be dead except for
his connections.

161

Most people expect more respect from others
than they give to themselves.

162

Success isn't the opposite of failure. A runner may
come in last, but if he beats his record, he succeeds.

163

Envy eats nothing but its own heart.

164

Don't be afraid to take a big step if one is indicated.
You can't cross a chasm in two small jumps.

165

Try to forget useless things. To remember
everything is to make your mind a dustbin.

166

Don't major in minor things.

167

Unless you are willing to come to your job
and be fired every day, you cannot do
your job properly!

WHEN YOU ARE FEELING
DOWN.
DON'T STAY THERE. DO SOMETHING.

168

Anger, like revenge, is a drink best served cold.
A little displeasure, in a low voice, should do
the trick. Difficult, but not impossible!

169

Follow no one but learn from everyone.

170

Management is a series of interruptions
interrupted by other interruptions!
Learn to reduce interruptions.

171

He who has good friends has no need for a mirror.

172

If you want to move mountains, you have to
first learn how to move particles.

173

If you do not make mistakes, it only means
you are not trying 100 per cent.

174

Take advice as you would take a sandwich—
with two big slices of doubt.

175

When it is impossible to change others,
you must change yourself.

176

We do things quickly to save time, and what do
we do with the extra time? We kill it!

YOU CAN'T CHANGE ANYONE.
YOU CAN'T CHANGE YOUR FATHER;
YOUR MOTHER, YOUR WIFE,
YOUR BROTHER, YOUR SISTER—
NOT EVEN YOUR BOSS!
CHANGE YOURSELF FIRST. PERIOD.

177

"My problem was I kept reading books on leadership
and excellence and management when I should
have been working."

178

Take three minutes to think of yourself first.

179

Winners develop the habit of doing the things that
losers don't like to do.

180

A man is not hurt so much by what happens,
as by his opinion of what has happened.

181

Work fewer hours; some of us waste half our time.

182

Don't do anything which someone else
can do for you.

183

Other men see things as they are and ask, "Why?"
I see things that never were and ask, "Why not?"

184

Don't say you don't have enough time.
You have exactly the same number of hours
per day that were given to Helen Keller,
Louis Pasteur, Michelangelo, Mother Teresa,
Leonardo da Vinci, Thomas Jefferson
and Albert Einstein.

If I had 8 hours to chop a tree I would spend 6 hours sharpening my axe.

The will to win is worthless if you do not have the will to prepare. Skyscrapers take only a year to build but many years to plan. And, patience in planning, impatience in execution has worked wonders.

185

Beaten paths are for beaten men.

186

A man's life is what his thoughts make of it.

187

Keep secrets.

188

Every thought we think is creating our future.

189

The wise man thinks before acting
and the fool thinks after it.

190

A change for the better always starts with
a change of thinking.

191

Where your mind goes your energy flows.

192

The more clear you are on what you want, the more
power you will have to achieve it.

193

Following a precedent is an easy
substitute for thinking.

194

A fundamental requirement for success: humility.

195

How many of us have realised that since we were
given two ears and one mouth it might be that we
were intended to listen twice as much as we speak?

WATCH YOUR THOUGHTS, THEY BECOME YOUR WORDS

WATCH YOUR WORDS, THEY BECOME YOUR ACTIONS

WATCH YOUR ACTIONS, THEY BECOME YOUR HABITS

WATCH YOUR HABITS, THEY BECOME YOUR CHARACTER

WATCH YOUR CHARACTOR, IT BECOME'S YOUR KARMA

196

I would rather sit on a pumpkin and have it all to
myself, than to be crowded on a velvet cushion.

197

You grow up the day you have your
first real laugh at yourself.

198

I believe in loyalty, for if I am not true to others,
I cannot be true to myself.

199

I believe in holding up my chin, for self-respect
commands respect from others.

200

For 25 years I tried to change my wife.
I could not do that. Then I thought for
25 minutes and decided to change myself.

201

I am changing myself, having fewer
expectations of others, not reacting
sharply to their behaviour.

202

The great pleasure in life is doing what people
say you cannot do.

203

Dare to dream — dare to try — dare to fail
dare to succeed.

2

Managing A Family

© Think Inc./Promod Batra

204

When your wife says she has a headache,
she may be saying that you are neglecting her.
Do not give her an aspirin.
The medicine required is flowers.

205

Spend more time in taking care of your sons and
daughters and converting them into assets — even if
both are liabilities to start with!

206

Life has become very complicated,
so please don't make it worse by
neglecting or overprotecting or overproviding
for your children.

207

The chemistry of each child,
like a customer or a client, is so
different that it is not funny. Be creative!

208

It is said that successful parents normally do not have
successful children. Prove it wrong.

209

Put yourself in your children's shoes. Let them be
known on their own and not as your children.
Give them opportunities to achieve small, small
successes. Don't push them. Do not insult
them by comparisons.

BE A BUDDY TO YOUR CHILDREN—DON'T BE JUST
A PARENT, BE A FRIEND! HOLD THEIR HANDS WHEN
THEY NEED COMFORTING, BUT WHEN NEEDED,
NUDGE THEM IN THE RIGHT DIRECTION!

210

You are your children's hero. Remember that.
Also remember that God has fitted the world's largest
and best video tape recorders in your children's
minds. The way you treat your parents, employees,
associates, customers; well, it is all getting taped to be
played back to you later!

211

Catch your child doing something right.
Helping him build a positive self-image is
one of the most important things you can do.

212

Proverbs contain the distilled wisdom of all ages!
Your sons and daughters won't have to invent
their own wheels. Books will give them a head start.
Encourage them to read non-fiction.

213

Use creativity when you want your children
to get into the habit of creativity.

214

Skipping college life may be a smart
thing but not wise.

215

Why do we want our children to grow up so fast that
they regret it when they look back?

216

Education is when your children can play
with their grandparents, their uncles, their friends.

Say "sorry" and make it up!
You will eliminate stress.

217

Help your children to take and make decisions.
Educate them with examples and stories.

218

Let your children spend a few days in a joint-family
system, a few days in a family where both
husband and wife work, a few days in
a big city, a few days in a small town,
and a few days on a farm and in a village.
This is also education.

219

Ensure that you have two-way communication
with your children. Remember that in two-way
communication it is not only the words but silence,
too, that can work miracles.

220

Don't be a preacher but a doer;
and do things to make
your children proud of you.

221

Try to be as honest and truthful and sincere as
possible. Even if your wife and your
children laugh at you, it is only outwardly.
Inside they will be proud of you.

222

Your child is always watching you and unless honesty,
truthfulness, and sincerity become your habits,
you do not have a chance of becoming
a hero in his eyes.

Take time off your busy business routine...
devote more time to your children.

223

As parents, do no: forget, you are leaders for
your sons and daughters! On leadership,
remember: "Don't Push: PULL."

224

As a leader, set objectives for your sons and
daughters such as becoming a doctor,
an engineer, an accountant,
a social worker and so on.
Keep on using the "dipstick" approach
observing and analysing which direction your
sons and daughters are going or are likely to go.

225

Whether your sons and daughters become assets or
liabilities, 70 per cent depends upon you
and 30 per cent on luck.

226

A pint can't hold a quart — if it holds a pint
it is doing all that can be expected of it.
(Each child has a different capacity!)

227

Don't be afraid to ask dumb questions; they're more
easily handled than dumb mistakes.

228

Did you ever hear of someone on
his death bed saying: "I wish I'd spent
more time at the office"?

229

Choose your life's mate carefully. From this one
decision will come sixty per cent of all your
happiness or misery.

230

Some parents scarcely bring up children;
they finance them.

231

The road to success is filled with women pushing
their husbands along.

232

The father who does not teach his son
his duties is as guilty as the son
who neglects them.

233

Don't dwell too long on the shortcomings of others.
Sure, your husband has faults. If he had been a saint,
he would never have married you. Right?

234

The only way to live in this world
is for every man to have a
fair-sized cemetery to bury the faults of others.

235

If your wife is your sleeping partner in business,
please wake her up. It will benefit you
both tremendously!

236

The best thing to spend on your children is your time.

By being over-protective,
you may be blocking your child's vision.

237

The way to get along is to go along.

238

If a thing is old, it is a sign that it was fit to live.
Old famiies, old customs, and old styles survive
because they are fit to survive.

239

Give your son a fish... he eats today.
Teach him how to fish... he eats everyday!

240

Why are we so polite to those we don't know,
and so rude and crude to those we love?

241

Remember that successful marriage
depends on two things:
(1) finding the right person, and
(2) being the right person.

242

A woman once asked Thomas A. Edison to write
a motto for her son. Edison wrote:
"Never look at the clock!"

243

If you keep the book too close to your eyes you can
only strain your eyes and not read the book.
Distance is required, also, between father and
son for the son to grow worldly-wise.

A good example is the best sermon.
It is equal to 10,000 words.

244

Normally, sons create and will continue to
create problems unless you plan or unless
they are smart enough!

245

The opportunity to do mischief is found a hundred
times a day and to do good, once in a year.

246

Mark Twain said in a tribute to his wife:
"Wherever she was, there was Eden."

247

Most businesses are inherited by inexperienced
children in the same way that children get
inexperienced parents!

248

Children are not born with an understanding of what
they can do or what they are worth to others.
They surely won't have any idea what the world
expects of them unless we make sure that they find
out. And they'll find this out best in the
hands of objective outsiders.

249

A family business is a serious business.
It cannot be conducted at the dinner table.

250

It is important to tell your son once in a while
when "enough is enough."

TEACH YOUR CHILDREN THE TRADE —
NOT THE TRICKS OF THE TRADE.

251

There is no single way but several
better ways which you can show to your son, and the
chances are that he will like a few of these.

252

Don't force your son to do what you want him to do.
He will then hate it. Let him decide himself, and you
will be surprised at his initiative.

253

Your son is like a body of flowing water.
You can regulate its flow by making small bunds;
you can then channelise the energies towards
the desired goal.

254

There is only a little less trouble in governing a son
than a whole kingdom.

255

One father is more than a hundred schoolmasters.

256

It really is impossible to please all the world and
your father, all the time.

3

Managing Friends

© Think Inc./Promod Batra

257

The only way to have a friend is to be one.

258

Be true to your word, your work, and your friend.

259

The most I can do for my friend is
simply to be his friend.

260

To suspect a friend is worse than to be
deceived by him.

261

Never injure a friend, even in jest.

262

No man is useless while he has a friend.

263

Life has no blessing like a prudent friend.

264

It is chance that makes brothers but
hearts that make friends.

265

Make new friends, but keep the old;
these are silver, those are gold.

266

The flower that follows the sun
does so even on cloudy days.

267

What is a friend? It is a person with
whom you dare to be yourself.

"Dot-ers"

On being asked by Akbar, Birbal painted the emperor's portrait in six days. Akbar asked his other eight Navratnas to comment. Each one put a dot on the portrait wherever he felt it was not good. Akbar asked Birbal to explain. Birbal thought and called for eight blank canvases for his colleagues and asked them to do the portrait. No one came forward. Akbar, with drooping eyes, murmured, "Dot-ers." MORAL: It is easy to find faults in what others do, but difficult to do it yourself.

268

A real friend never gets in your way unless
you happen to be on the way down.

269

Never develop a friendship with a man
who is not better than yourself.

270

A little straight talk between friends is sometimes the
best way to stay friends.

271

You can hardly make a friend in a year,
but you can lose one in an hour.

272

A fallen enemy may rise again, but the reconciled
one is truly vanquished.

273

It is not as difficult to die for a friend,
as to find a friend worth dying for.

274

Have you fifty friends? It is not enough.
Have you one enemy? It is too much.

275

Friendship improves happiness, and abates misery,
by doubling our joy, and dividing our grief.

276

The language of friendship is not words but meanings.
It is an intelligence above language.

277

Two persons cannot long be friends if they cannot
forgive each other's little failings.

278

God evidently does not intend us all to be rich,
or powerful, or great, but he does intend
us all to be friends.

279

The firmest friendships have been formed in mutual
adversity, as iron is most strongly united by
the fiercest flames.

280

All men have their frailties and whoever looks for
friends without imperfections will never find
what he seeks.

281

A sorrow shared is a sorrow halved.

282

Don't walk in front of me, I may not follow.
Don't walk behind me, I may not lead.
Walk beside me and just be my friend.

283

Three days of uninterrupted company in a vehicle
will make you better friends than one hour's
conversation every day for three years.

284

Develop friendships with people having
twenty-twenty vision.

285
He is a good friend that speaks well of us
behind our backs.

286
Trust not a new friend or an old enemy.

287
Never say you know a friend till you have divided
an inheritance with him.

288
A good neighbour doubles the value of a house.

289
What upsets me is not that your
lied to me but that from now onwards
I can no longer believe you.

290
Your friend is the man who knows all about you,
and still likes you!

291
Prosperity makes friends and adversity tries them.

292
God send me a friend who will tell me of my faults.

293
Books and friends' should be few and good.

294
Don't burn bridges. You'll be surprised how
many times you have to cross the same river.

4

Managing Employees

AN ORGANISATION IS A UNION OF
ORDINARY PEOPLE DOING
EXTRA ORDINARY WORK

295

Too many people are thinking of security
instead of opportunity. They seem more afraid
of life than of death.

296

When all of us think alike, no one is thinking.

297

Never hire anyone who will work for money alone.

298

When the blind man carries the lame,
both go forward.

299

When you need 2.5 people, hire the second one.

300

Helping people helps in the long run.

301

When we educate ourselves, we build the
power to accomplish our goals.

302

Don't keep a dog and bark yourself.

303

Praise in public; reprimand in private.

304

Remember that nobody is a nobody.

305

If you ignore substandard work,
it becomes acceptable.

Respect skill.

An American was travelling in Afghanistan when his Cadillac stalled. He did everything, but it didn't start. Finally, a mechanic came from the hills riding a donkey. He opened the bonnet and hit the cylinder head six times. He asked the American to start it and it did. The American asked, "How much?" The mechanic said, "$100." The American gasped and asked him to itemise the bill. The mechanic said, "10¢ for hitting six times and $99.90 for knowing where to hit." MORAL: Respect skilled people.

306

A manager creates conditions for
his people to achieve results.

307

A manager shows his greatness by
the way he treats little employees.

308

I will speak ill of no man, and speak all
the good I know of everybody.

309

The man who trusts men will make fewer
mistakes than he who distrusts them.

310

Those who only do what they are told
are seldom told to do anything.

311

It ain't what you say,
it's the way that you say it that gets results.

312

When you kill somebody's good idea,
you kill a little of that person too.

313

Use meetings and conferences for
cross-pollination of better ways.

314

Don't tell me how hard you work;
tell me how much you get done.

THERE ARE GOOD MEN EVERYWHERE.
I ONLY WISH THEY HAD LOUDER VOICES.

315

If you were a dairy farmer, would you employ twice
as many milkers as cows?

316

Never hire your friends.
Never hire your client's children.
Never hire your own children.

317

Whenever you get medals, give them to your
colleagues You will get more.

318

Do a kindness once and it will be seen as a favour;
do it twice, and it becomes a duty.

319

Hating people is like burning down
your own house to get rid of a rat.

320

Coming together is a beginning; keeping together is
progress; working together is success.

321

You can preach a better sermon
with your life than with your lips.

322

Don't run down the other man's plans
unless you have better ones to offer.

323

A committee is a thing which takes a week to
do what one good man can do in an hour.

If you offer peanuts, you will get monkeys!

Pay well, a cheap employee is expensive. The best executive is the one who has the good sense to pick good men to do what he wants done, and enough self-restraint to keep from meddling with them while they do it.

The secret of his success was the ability to attract exceptionally able men and to treat them with so much respect that they never left.

324

A man should live with his superiors as he
does with fire—not too near,
lest he burn, nor too far off, lest he freeze.

325

A suggestion box can work as well in a business with
six employees as in a company with 1000 employees.

326

Working together not only brings out the best in all of
us; it brings out the best in each one of us.

327

Remember that a person's name is to that person the
sweetest and most important sound in any language.

328

The difference between a secretary and a professional
secretary is in keeping your balance when everything
was needed yesterday.

329

If we decide to negotiate, then we must be open
to compromise.

330

Your mind is like a camera with memory! It can take
pictures which you can "file" for subsequent use.

331

The German army won't let a soldier file a
complaint or make a criticism immediately after
a thing has happened.

332

Throughout history there have been two categories
of people: those who create wealth and
those who consume it.

333

People who accept responsibility are the people
who are making the most of their lives.

334

If you observe people long enough,
you'll realise that the self-made ones have
an abundance of working parts.

335

If each of us hires people who are
smaller than we are,
we shall become a company of dwarfs.
But if each of us hires people who are
bigger than we are,
we shall become a company of giants.

336

In your job or at your house, you are a member of an
orchestra. It depends upon you whether the result
is music or noise.

337

Listen to what your employees say. Very often, their
ideas are like burning embers. You can kindle them
into fires, or reduce them to ashes with a few drops
of cold water in the form of judgment.

Here are 10 tried and tested ways to kill the good ideas and enthusiasm of your co-workers.

1. It's against company policy.
2. It doesn't fit the system.
3. It will never be approved.
4. The timing just isn't right.
5. It didn't work before.
6. It's too wild.
7. We're not ready for that.
8. I will think about it.
9. Put something in writing and get back to me.
10. Let's form a committee.

338

From softness arises humility.
From humility arises trust.
From trust arises togetherness and one mind.

339

Everyone has dreams. It is not your job to
go around bursting dreams.

340

Anyone can live by working 8 to 5, but success is
achieved by working from 5 to 8.

341

Before you point a finger at your employee,
use the "dipstick" on yourself as to
how honest you are with your customers.

342

Personally I am very fond of strawberries and
cream, but I find that for some strange reason
fish prefer worms. So when I go fishing,
I don't think about what I want;
I think about what they want.

343

Your mind is like an acre of land.
Look after it! Hard work is like tilling;
good reading acts like fertilizer;
discipline is like pesticides.

344

Feel like a hero every day by doing a good deed
for your employees.

345

Do not be angry that you cannot make others
as you wish them to be since you cannot make
yourself as you wish to be.

346

Some people think they are generous
because they give away free advice.

347

Your mind is the best asset you have.
The minds of your employees are the "assets"
which do not appear in your balance sheet.

348

To keep customers, business needs to invest
in its employees.

349

Everybody wants to succeed.
Give them a fair chance.

350

There is always more to learn and more to earn
for every employee.

351

We learn a lot by listening to our employees
because, after all, wisdom is not the
exclusive possession of management.

352

People don't waste time.
They just spend it on things
they don't need to do.

Training that brings about no change is as effective as a parachute that opens on the first bounce.

353

Wise men learn by others' mistakes,
fools by their own.

354

Relax ! Relax ! Relax ! Learn to relax while you are
doing your work!

355

There are two sides to every issue, so make certain
you keep both your ears open and listening.

356

People are sick of getting letters that sound like
they have been written by a computer
that knows their name.

357

There's little choice among rotten apples.

358

Treating people courteously
requires very little effort.

359

Please all and you please none.

360

Good leadership starts with good
communication with people.

361

As I grow older, I pay less attention to what
men say. I just watch what they do.

362

A boss has to be a good shock absorber.

NO MATTER HOW MUCH WORK A MAN CAN DO,
NO MATTER HOW ENGAGING HIS PERSONALITY
MAY BE, HE WILL NOT ADVANCE FAR
IN BUSINESS IF HE CANNOT WORK ALONG
WITH OTHERS.

363

Conduct meetings with your managers in your head
before meeting them across the table.

364

There is no easy way to dress up someone's
performance without dressing him down.

365

A man will not sell his life to you, but he will
give it to you for a piece of coloured ribbon.
Grant ribbons.

366

The administrator may have to stay
out of the way in order to get his way.

367

Loosen up. Except for rare life-and-death matters,
nothing is as important as it first seems.

368

A projecting nail must be hammered down.

369

A soft voice is heard long after the shout.
Gentleness is stronger than anger.

370

As a manager you're paid to be uncomfortable.
If you're comfortable, it's a sure sign that
you're doing things wrong.

371

Sound becomes music if a trained man makes it.
Training is essential.

Do you encourage yes men?

372

You cannot train a horse with shouts and
expect it to obey a whisper.

373

You cannot teach new tricks to an old dog. True.
But you and I are not dogs.

374

Never try to teach a pig to sing. It wastes your
time and annoys the pig.

375

Find out whether it is ignorance or indifference.
Ignorance is easy to remove by education and training.
Indifference needs creativity to be removed.

376

Communicate downward to subordinates with
at least the same care and attention as you
communicate upward to superiors.

377

The best leaders lead by demonstrating
how it is done.

378

Asking costs little.

379

Condemn actions, not people.

380

Criticism dispensed in small doses rather than
large ones is a lot easier on a person's ego and
is far more productive.

The ups and downs of life are all in books. Someone, somewhere, sometime has had your problems and opportunities. You don't have to invent your own wheel.

381

Delegate but don't forget.

382

Demand and you will get it, i.e. extraordinary
performance from the average man or from yourself.

383

Different strokes for different folks.

384

What matters most today is the
ability to think together.

385

The hard and unbending are broken by change;
the supple and yielding make way and prevail.

386

It is true that we learn by listening,
yet we don't listen.

387

Teach, don't preach.

388

Listening is an art. Listen with your eyes also.

389

Few persons weigh the faults of others
without a thumb on the scales.

390

If you can't explain what you're doing by
using simple language, you are probably doing
something wrong.

391

Everyone is a trainee as well as a trainer.

392

Everyone needs training—
from a prime minister to a peon.

393

Managing your business is an art and not a science.

394

Training demands patience and persistence.

395

Anybody can become angry—that is easy; but to be
angry with the right person, to the right degree,
at the right time, and for the right purpose —
that is certainly not easy.

396

It is more fun to be overworked than
to be underworked.

397

It requires more common sense to get
work done than to do it

398

Training demands a positive attitude.

399

Training is expensive to impart as well as to receive.

400

Never allow two people to do a job
which only one can do.

There is no indispensable man.

Sometime when you're feeling important;
Sometime when your ego's in bloom,
Sometime when you take it for granted
You're the best qualified in the room,
Sometime when you feel that your going
Would leave an unfillable hole,
Just follow these simple instructions
And see how they humble your soul:

Take a bucket and fill it with water,
Put your hand in it up to the wrist,
Pull it out and the hole that's remaining
Is a measure of how you'll be missed.
You can splash all you wish when you enter,
You may stir up the water galore,
But stop and you'll find that in no time
It looks quite the same as before.

The moral of this quaint example
Is do just the best that you can.
Be proud of yourself but remember,
There's no indispensable man.

401

Working together won't work if you do not take to
task anyone who doesn't carry his share of the load.

402

No rebuke is so powerful as the
influence of a good example.

403

Nothing makes a person's chest stick out further
than being asked his opinion on a subject
he knows is of special importance to the questioner.
It makes one feel one's judgment is valued.

404

Working together works, and with a smile, working
together works faster, better, smoother.

405

Honor and rank are nothing more than
gulls resting on the water.

406

Firmness with fairness and
quickness tones up a team.

407

People want to work and
they want to work purposefully.

408

People work for satisfaction.
They work for challenge and recognition.
Money, yes, buys their hands.
The rest buys their heads and hearts.

DON'T MAKE BEST THE ENEMY OF BETTER

Many times we forget the "better" in our quest for the "best." If we implement "better," in nine out of ten cases it would lead us to "still better." Why go far for an example if you are a married person? Think of your spouse. Is he or she the best person, the ideal you had desired before getting married? Yes? Maybe you think so now. Good for your marital bliss. But, be sure. Didn't you make some compromise somewhere in looks, habits or profession? The point is: had you waited to get the "best" spouse, you would have definitely remained unmarried throughout your life.

Remember: GOOD, BETTER, BEST. Always start with GOOD and implement it. Next, try to improve it. Try to do BETTER and still BETTER. Make it an on-going process to do the BEST.

409

Don't be deceived by first impressions.

410

Never be vindictive with anyone; forgive and forget.

411

Start measuring your people by the size of their
thinking — not only in kilograms and inches !

412

A wound inflicted by speech is more painful
than a wound inflicted by the sword.

413

Trust is like a chain of thought. Once you break it,
it is almost impossible to put it together again.

414

Situations themselves do not cause stress;
your reactions do.

415

Do not take it for granted that working together
works automatically. You have to keep on
"repairing the fences" to keep your
business in good condition.

416

When big bells ring, no one hears the small ones.

417

When management arrives before the workforce and
leaves after they do, they are seen as
providing leadership.

Admit your mistakes gracefully.

Even the chairman's pencil has an eraser on it. We all make mistakes. Do not be afraid of admitting mistakes. We cannot be right all the time. The man who is right only 60 per cent of the time can be a howling success if he is quick to correct his mistakes the rest of the time. The best thing is, people really respect a man who admits his mistakes quickly and gracefully. It is the mark of a big man.

418

An administrator must be adept at adapting.

419

When you want to get things done, use creative ways
to remind people. Don't forget that people tend to
forget conveniently.

420

Accept praise with humility. Don't forget that,
backstage, you have a whole lot of team-mates who
helped you achieve all that you have.

421

Understand the Pygmalion effect. Or the "Holi" way—
i.e. if you spray scented water on other people,
they will do the same to you. And if you smear them
with dirty water, they will do that to you, too.

422

Shout...whenever you are reasonably sure that
someone in the team is over- or
under-carrying the load!

423

A manager's success is due 15 per cent to technical
skills and 85 per cent to skills in human engineering.

424

Good managers are not born,
they are obtained by training.

425

Most people remember only
20 per cent of what they hear.

STARVE
THE
PROBLEMS
FEED
THE
OPPORTUNITIES

426

Never stop listening; never stop learning;
never stop training.

427

Start treating your people as grown-ups. Give them
responsibility and authority. Trust them.

428

Never be too busy to say nice words to your people
whenever they do something good.
Go out of your way to find such opportunities.

429

The rapidity with which we forget is astonishing.

430

Do you show enthusiasm, initiative, loyalty,
devotion to your business and your people?
If you do, you will get it from your people, too.

431

Upgrading your people is a far more challenging job
than upgrading yourself or your facilities.

432

Delays make people lose interest and become lazy.

433

A ballet dancer needs a mirror to perfect her style and
technique. A manager needs to develop his own mirror.

434

A man who climbs to the peak foot by foot earns
far more respect than the one who
reaches there by helicopter.

Madan Agarwal's maxim...

" Everyone likes to do what he likes and not what should be done "

It is a common phenomenon in offices. You ask your colleague to do something and just when you are expecting the results, you discover that he has been at something else just because he liked doing what he liked and did not do what should have been done.

Why do individuals behave so? Part of human nature. . . maybe.

Looked at the other way round, why does one behave contrary to how we expect one to behave? Well, children like to do what they are prevented from doing. But it happens with elders when they are not properly guided. And more important, when they are not properly motivated.

435

A person's true character is often revealed by the manner in which he receives praise.

436

Give editorial freedom to a nightingale and you will get a song of summer in full-throated ease. Give it to a pig and you will get a grunt.

437

Give someone a title and you make a hundred people angry and one person ungrateful.

438

He gives twice who gives quickly.

439

He who wants to eat the fruit must climb the tree.

440

He travels fastest who travels alone.

441

If you want to get a thing done, give it to the busiest executive.

442

Any person who enjoys responsibility usually gets it.

443

The best of men is he who sees his own faults and does not see the faults of others.

444

Everything takes longer than you think. So add "10 to 30%" before you give a target date.

Skills aren't enough;
it's your attitude
that makes the
difference

445

The squeaking wheel gets the grease.

446

The used key is always bright.

447

There is nothing so powerful as the truth.

448

There is no such thing as a perfect solution.

449

These hackneyed proverbs contain the
very essence of the distilled
wisdom of all ages.

450

Thirty per cent of your employees are lazy,
stupid, dishonest and so on.
Take this factor into your calculations.

451

Throw enough dirt, and some will stick.

452

Walk 25% faster, and you will feel not only
smarter but will impress other people.
Try it.

453

An appraisal system is no good without
an effective grievances processing system.

454

Positive and negative strokes
should be well mixed.

DO IMPORTANT JOBS NOW BEFORE THEY BECOME URGENT

Procrastination is the thief of time.

The habit of putting off important tasks can rob you of hours of achievement and success.

Do not forget, the world's biggest fires could have been prevented by a small cup of water. And, a telegram results when a postcard isn't sent.

Why neglect the job at hand now and let it crush you under its weight later? A stitch in time saves nine. Attack the task with full gusto and you will be pleasantly surprised at your own competence.

A thousand mile journey begins with a single step. Take the step. Leave inertia behind. See the miles melt away under your feet. Do it now!

© Think Inc./Promod Batra

455

Leadership is like moving a string.
You cannot move it by pushing from behind;
what you have to do is to get ahead and pull.

456

The reason many people fail to recognise opportunity
is because it comes disguised as hard work.

457

The least important word in social
and congregational life is "I"
and the most important word is "You."

458

Work smarter, not just harder!

459

It is good to become a hero in films,
but not in the business world!
Ensure that your team becomes the hero.

460

Jobs don't have futures; people do.

461

People are seldom angry for the reason they think
they are angry. There is usually something else
at the bottom of it.

462

Encourage people to suggest possible solutions to
each problem that they put up.

463

Treat people like winners.

Think people,
Good people,
Committed people.

One way to encourage excellence is to demand excellence. Very often, you will get it! Notice it. Say a nice word about it. Talk about it. Write about it. But, always, praise in public, reprimand in private.

You can get more work done with a kind word and a gun than a kind word alone! And, remember, nothing motivates a man more than to see his boss putting in an honest day's work.

464

If you want to plan for a year, plant corn.
If you want to plan for three years, plant a tree.
But if you want to plan for ten years, plant men.

465

People can be divided into three groups — those who
make things happen; those who watch things happen;
and those who wonder what happened.

466

Good people without discipline are worth nothing.

467

See the good in people and try to develop those
qualities.

468

Inefficiency: if it cannot be overcome and an employee
is obviously incapable of the job, find a job he can do
or dismiss him now. Don't wait.

469

Don't try to do an employee's job for him —
counsel and suggest.

470

We do not hire a man's history, we hire the man.

471

The people you may have with you may not be the
best; how you use them decides your profits.

472

A good leader leads the group with the flag in his
hand. He does not have to shout.

PERFECTION IS PARALYSIS..

473

People do judge you by the way you speak!

474

Computers do not make mistakes; people do.

475

You can have the best seeds in the world,
but if your seed bed is not prepared properly
germination will not take place.

476

Don't expect others to listen to your advice
and ignore your example.

477

People are not against you;
they are merely for themselves.

478

Those who are pulling on the oars don't
have much time to rock the boat.

479

What takes one guy one hour to do
will take two guys two hours to do.

480

Nothing provides more leisure time than a
number of capable assistants.

481

Never give a man up until he has failed at
something he likes.

THE SILENCE OF PURE INNOCENCE
PERSUADES WHEN SPEAKING FAILS.
— William Shakespeare

482

Lessons are not given, they are taken.

483

The first problem for all of us, men and women,
is not to learn but to unlearn.

484

Men are never attached to you by favours.

485

Forgive many things in others, nothing in yourself.

486

A little friction is often needed to get traction.

487

The best way to get things done is to allow your
subordinates to formulate their own methods of
operation.

488

A man who cannot tolerate small ills can never
accomplish great things.

489

It appears on close examination that
work is less boring than amusing onself.

490

Far and away the best prize that life offers is the
chance to work hard at something worth doing.

491

The difference between a job and a career is the
difference between 40 and 60 hours a week.

Let us learn from a humble *madariwala*. He does his job very well and is stressfree because he focuses on one ball at a time.

492

There are plenty of employees who have
retired on the job.

493

The best career advice given to the young is,
"Find out what you like doing best and get someone
to pay you for doing it."

494

When a stupid man is doing something he is ashamed
of, he always declares that it is his duty.

495

Duty largely consists of pretending that
the trivial is critical.

496

When you have a number of disagreeable duties to
perform, always do the most disagreeable first.

497

You can't hold a man down without staying
down with him.

498

Too many people stop looking for work
when they find a job.

499

The secret principle of human nature is
the craving to be appreciated.

500

Working with people is difficult,
but not impossible.

The Boss Is Always Right

WHAT THE PEOPLE SAY	FOR ME...	FOR MY BOSS...
When one talks...	I am talkative	He is social.
When one mixes with people...	I am going in for cheap popularity.	He is gregarious.
When one goes early...	I abuse concession.	It is an adjustment.
When one mixes with ladies...	I am always after women.	He is charming.
When one gets up late...	I am lazy.	He was working late last night.
When one corrects others...	I am showing off.	He is guiding others.
When cases are kept pending...	I am incompetent.	He is diplomatic.
When a job takes a long time...	I am slow.	He is thorough.
When a job is not done...	I am lethargic.	He is too busy.
When a mistake is made...	I am careless.	He is human.
When a job is done without being told...	I am overstepping my responsibilities.	He has initiative.
When a stand is taken...	I am bull-headed.	He is firm.
When a rule etiquette is overlooked...	I am rude.	He is being original.
When progress is made...	I get breaks.	He has worked hard.
When one rises to an occasion...	I am an opportunist.	He will definitely do it.
When a lottery is won...	I am avaricious.	He is always lucky.
When one goes for a walk...	I am loitering.	He takes care of his health.

☐ Think Inc./Promod Batra

501

You can't have everything in one person.

502

The great composer does not set to work because he is
inspired, but becomes inspired because he is working.
He didn't waste time waiting for inspiration.

503

If you want something done,
give it to a busy executive, and
he'll have his secretary do it.

504

The businessman is coming to realise that education is
to business what fertilizer is to farming.

505

Be moderate in praising a man when he is present,
but give him full credit when he is absent.

506

The frog tried to look like the elephant...
and burst.

507

The sparrow feels sorry for the peacock
because of the burden on its tail!

508

The mob has many heads,
but no brains.

509

Great people are attracted to great leaders.
Great managers end up working for great people.

One man makes the difference...

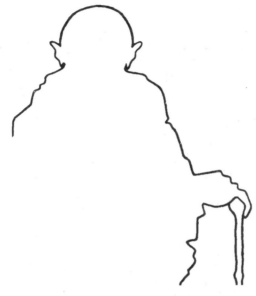

The word "Leader" comes from "Lord" which meant, in Old Norse, the course or path of a ship at sea. The leader was the captain, who in Viking days was usually the steersman and navigator as well.

Now, whether one is the leader of a nation, of a business, of a department, or of a home, one has to have the following:

- The ability to think deeply.
- The ability to communicate effectively.
- The ability to foresee the future and take necessary corrective action from time to time.
- The ability to make things happen.

The image and character of any group are reflections of the image and character of its leader. . . the man who makes all the difference.

© Think Inc./Promod Batra

510

Excellence in action in an organisation is
when employees: pay attention to details, do things
right the first time, and practice good human relations.

511

People tend to look upon successful people as they
appear now. They overlook the many years of hard
work, failure, frustrations, and problems —
all encountered, lots conquered — all along the way.

512

In order for people to be happy in their work
three things are needed:
(1) They must be fit for it.
(2) They must not do too much of it.
(3) And they must have a sense of success in it.

513

If you're the boss and your people fight you openly
when they think you're wrong — that's healthy.
If your men fight each other openly in your presence
for what they believe in — that's healthy.
But keep all the conflict eyeball to eyeball.

5

Managing Customers

A SMILE IS THE UNIVERSAL LANGUAGE WHICH IS UNDERSTOOD, AROUND THE WORLD...

514

If you take care of your staff,
your staff will take care of your customers.

515

Mean what you say.

516

Any successful organisation has
the customer as its focus.

517

The more prospects you meet,
the more customers you get.

518

"Maybe the customer is right" works wonders.

519

Agreement with customers gets
better results than arguments.

520

The only way to get the best of
an argument with a customer is to avoid it.

521

Think of the customer first if you want the
customer to think of you first.

522

Every customer is essential
to the well-being of the organisation.

523

You never get a second chance to
make a good first impression.

WHY CUSTOMERS QUIT

1%. DIE

3%. MOVE AWAY

5%. FORM OTHER FRIENDSHIPS

9%. FOR COMPETITIVE REASONS

14%. BECAUSE OF PRODUCT DISSATISFACTION

68%. BECAUSE OF AN ATTITUDE OF INDIFFERENCE ON THE PART OF AN EMPLOYEE.

524

Small opportunities are often the beginning
of great enterprises.

525

The more liberal a refund policy a business has,
the more likely it will be able to avoid disgruntled
and unhappy customers.

526

There are really two entries to be made
for every transaction: one in terms
of immediate currency and coin,
the other in terms of goodwill.

527

"Kiss" your customers. Keep it simple.
When Banta Singh walks into your showroom, tell
him, "You can send your son to college on
the money you save on an Escorts tractor."

528

Ninety per cent of your customers are reasonable;
it is only 10 per cent of them who require
tactful handling.

529

Always exceed the customer's expectations.

530

A rupee goes a long way now.
You can carry it around for days without
finding a thing it will buy.

THE CUSTOMER IS THE BOSS

There never has been... there is not now... and there never will be any boss but the customer. **He** is the one boss you must please. Everything you own... **he** has paid for. **He** buys your home, your cars, your clothes. **He** pays for your vacations and puts your children through school. **He** will give you every promotion you will ever obtain during your lifetime... and **he** will discharge you if you displease him.

—*Earl Nightingale*

531

A customer, like anyone else, may not be able to
take and make decisions easily. Once you give him
the alternatives and educate him on how to take a
decision and do not push him, he is likely to
choose the alternative that will make him happy.

532

Treat your customers' complaints as suggestions!

533

Be more prompt to go to your customer in
adversity than to the one in prosperity.

534

They also serve their customers who only stand and
wait for the customer to come in!

535

Feel like a hero every day by doing
a good deed for your customer.

536

Be selfish but be honest to your customers!

537

Business exists only to create customers, more
customers and many, many more customers.

538

Consumers are statistics; customers are business.

539

Customers forget very quickly;
therefore give fast service.

540

Customers are not hard to please.

541

Make yours a customer-oriented business.

542

If you run after two hares, you catch neither.

543

Customer satisfaction is affordable and profitable
because a satisfied customer becomes
your salesman forever.

544

Customers want answers to their problems; they are
not impressed by your carpets and chandeliers.

545

Do not so over-welcome the new customers
as to annoy the old ones.

546

Each of your employees should visit your customers.
Even accounts people. Follow-up on complaints and
suggestions is a must.

547

The essence of marketing is to create customers;
profits will follow.

548

Bait the hook to suit the fish.

549

Get the customer to do most of the talking.
The more you listen, the wiser he thinks you are.

A satisfied customer is your best advertisement.

A sale is not a one-time transaction — it is the beginning of repeat business provided you keep the customer satisfied. And there is no other way of doing it than to be prompt in reaching out to him in his adversity and giving him good after-sales service.

No amount of advertising — leaflets, banners, hoardings, wall paintings, newspaper and magazine insertions, radio jingles, television advertisement films — have the credibility which a satisfied customer has.

If you are sincere in helping him and create in him the confidence that you are always behind him, you will see the word of mouth spread like wildfire. Not only will he give you repeat business, he will get you the business of his friends and acquaintances too.

550

Give the customers the best you have and the
customers will give you back the best they have.

551

He pleases customers best,
who trusts customers most.

552

Honesty is still the best policy,
with common sense,
with your customers.

553

If you are not busy meeting customers,
you're forcing them to
visit your competitors.

554

It costs six times as much to get a new customer as to
keep a customer you already have.

555

It is natural for your customers to
forget to be grateful; so if you go
around expecting gratitude, you are
heading straight for a lot of heartaches.

556

Judge a customer more by his
questions than by his answers.

557

Keep on checking with your key customers
about your employees. Do it discreetly.

Ask the customer...

In a company meeting, everybody was giving suggestions on how to make better dog food. On being asked by the chairman, a trainee suggested, "Sir, I am not a dog. Let us get a few dogs to the conference table and put out different food formula specimens, and make the one they like." MORAL: Ask the customer what he needs.

558

It is one of the most beautiful
compensations of this life that no
man can sincerely try to
help another without helping himself.

559

Learn to listen.
Opportunity sometimes knocks very softly.

560

Nothing motivates a customer more than
to see his dealer putting in an honest
day's work to solve his problems.

561

Nurture your customers !

562

One small deed for your customer accomplishes
more than a thousand words.

563

One way to be popular with your customers is
to remember a nice thing a customer said
about some other customer
and tell him.

564

Poorly served employees serve
customers just as poorly.

EVERYTHING ELSE IS
OVERHEAD!

The customer is not an inconvenience or a pain in the neck. He is our bread and butter. He pays for our salaries and our profits.

The customer is the only goose that lays golden eggs every day... forever! So care for him, pamper him. Sow the best possible service and reap a golden harvest. . . in bumper profits.

A company sailing with a heavy load of overhead will soon find itself at the bottom. Axe the overhead. And, make it a monthly exercise, not yearly. Eliminate those activities which are not for the customers, the real boss.

565

Present customers are and will continue to be
the best prospects for more business !
Spend time and effort to read your present
customers accurately, tune in to what they
require in terms of assistance and support.
Do not take them for granted.

566

Customers are innovative by nature
and will always opt for the better.

567

Some customers simply cost more to serve.
It makes good business sense.

568

There are sunrise and sunset customers...
watch out and learn the difference.

569

You cannot expect your employees to be honest
if you cheat your customers.

570

The buyer has need of a hundred eyes;
the seller of but one.

571

There is no such thing as "soft sell" and
"hard sell." There is only "smart sell"
and "stupid sell."

THE COST IS LONG FORGOTTEN BUT THE

UALITY

IS REMEMBERED FOREVER.

572

Unless you are willing to come to your business daily
thinking that your customers are going to desert you,
you cannot manage your business for profit.

573

Very little is needed to make your
customers happy.

574

We must adjust ourselves to the customers —
never the customers to ourselves.

575

When things go wrong with a customer, as they
sometimes will, rest if you must, but don't quit.

576

The realisation of losing a customer expresses
the determination to gain another one
by working hard all over again.

577

When your customer says he has a big problem,
he may in fact be saying that you are neglecting him.
Do not give him free service or discounts.
He needs to be listened to more.

578

Winning a new account is a heady experience,
but losing one is pure hell.
What do you do to convince your other customers that
they too should not dismiss you?

The time has come to put yourself in your customer's shoes.

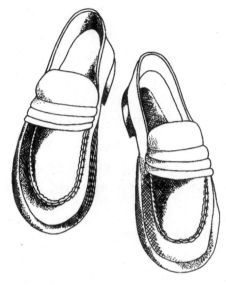

Should we tell you the secret of success? Find a need and fill it!

Once you've identified customer needs and satisfied them, you're in possession of the magic wand that will conjure up fabulous fortunes. But, how do you know what the customer wants?

By seeing things his way, that's how! What would you want, if you were in his place? Find that out. And set out to satisfy it as if your life depends on it. (At least your success in business depends on it, does it not?)

"If there is any secret of success," says Henry Ford, "it lies in the ability to get the other person's point of view and see things from his angle..."

579

With annoyed customers, the policy of "I will try" has done wonders.

580

You get your accounts audited.
Do you get your customers audited?

581

Our customers are our very best friends.

582

Spread a smile and make profits.

583

Discipline results in faster customer service.

584

Communication with the customer is
the core of good customer service.
Everyone in business "communicates" with
customers. Therefore, train each of
your employees to be a good listener,
to be patient and to express himself clearly.

585

You have not converted a man just because
you have silenced him.

586

Customers like to feel good about themselves no
matter what they are doing. They want to think of
themselves as intelligent, wise and competent beings.
They do not want to think of themselves as foolish.

Handle a difficult customer with care.

A difficult customer is a dark cloud with a silver lining. He is your golden opportunity to prove your mettle as a sales person. Win him over and you have sharpened your technique of satisfying customers and getting more business.

Handle a difficult customer with tact and sympathy. Put yourself in his shoes and see where it pinches. Then mend it. Remove the irritations to make him happy.

See him walk out with a smile on his face. And, you may rest assured, he will get you a hundred more customers.

587

Your attitude determines the
satisfaction level of your customers.

588

Excellence is when a man asks of
himself more than others do.

589

It is impossible to make a
good deal with bad people.

590

The basic philosophy of any business,
particularly a service business,
is to do two things: get and keep customers.

591

Rewarding employees for friendliness
toward customers reinforces
the feeling that the customers come first.

592

Instill in your mind that we offer better, far better
service to our customers than our competition does.
Only half of our job is selling our services;
the other half is servicing our customers.

593

Studies have shown that 96 per cent of the customers
who are dissatisfied with an organization's
services don't actually complain.

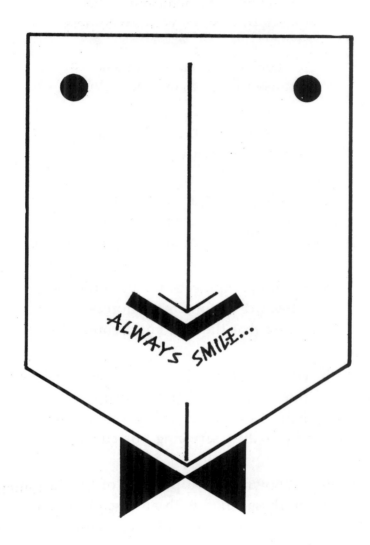

594

If you are not hearing customer complaints,
that doesn't mean that everything is okay.
It may only mean that uncomplaining customers are
quietly accepting conditions they dislike and
planning never to return.

595

When you do hear complaints, you have a second
chance to make things right, to improve conditions,
not only for a specific customer, but for all those other
customers who follow.

596

Sometimes the things we don't say speak louder than
the things we do say. Looking annoyed, fidgeting,
appearing rushed, avoiding eye contact, continuing to
attend to paperwork — all these non-verbal
behaviours turn customers off!

597

Customers who write or call with complaints want
someone to listen, sympathise, apologise,
and, if indicated, correct the matter.

6

Managing   Competition

598

If you can't stand the competition,
get out of the business.

599

If you go through the wars, you get the medals.

600

Success doesn't depend upon being at the right place
at the right time; it depends upon being ready.

601

Of two heroes, he is greater who
esteems his rivals most.

602

Nothing happens unless we make it
happen in the bazaar.

603

No one puts out other people's lamps.
It is the lack of oil which puts them out.

604

Why are we shocked when success brings
us more problems than it solves?
We are surprised by the obvious.

605

If you play safe in life, you've decided that
you don't want to grow anymore.

606

The best of all ways to beat competition is, of course,
to serve your customers better.

SHAPE UP OR SHIP OUT

Today, the world is moving at supersonic speed. Things are changing at a frantic pace. Only razor-sharp reflexes can help you respond to each new challenge and be on the top.

Keep yourself fighting fit! Absorb every new idea. And be alert to every minute change. Or else, your competitors will leave you light years behind. Today, business is like riding a bicycle—either you keep moving or you fall down. And sink into oblivion.

Now, spur yourself on. And move up. Keep on keeping on! There's plenty of room at the top but there's no room to sit down.

607

Love your competitor, it'll drive him crazy.
Don't criticise him;
he is just what you would be
under similar circumstances.

608

If you have too many problems,
maybe you should go out of business.
There is no law that says a company
must exist forever.

609

If your mousetraps are better than those of others,
people will beat a path to you
wherever you are — even in the forest.

610

When starting out, don't worry about not having
enough money. Limited funds are a blessing,
not a curse. Nothing encourages creative
thinking in quite the same way.

611

It is our policy not to compete in price with any
competitor. We manufacture quality products
and sell them, and not the price.

612

Price doesn't matter if you make the buyer
want the thing more than... the price.

If you are not busy meeting competition, you are creating it.

Competition is not an enemy which has to be feared. Meet it halfway and accept the challenge. One way to beat the competition is to serve your customers better. We have strengths and we have weaknesses. But so have our competitors. And, if we sell our strengths against their weaknesses, we will win.

613

If a thing is worth doing,
it's worth doing well.

614

Statistics are no substitute for judgment.

615

Quality is really a way of managing an organisation.

616

The system, not the workers, causes
the great majority of quality problems.

617

Place quality before profits.

618

Only those who can give 'the best for the least' will
survive, and others will be for sale.

619

Your business will be a 'rice bowl' or a 'rust bowl'
depending on your attitude today.

620

The competitor who won a customer from you might
broadcast his victory to all who will listen.

621

The more people trust you,
the more people buy from you.

622

Harmony, aesthetics and beauty are found
in the simplest things.

THE ULTIMATE MEASURE OF A MAN
IS NOT WHERE HE STANDS IN MOMENTS OF
COMFORT AND CONVENIENCE,
BUT WHERE HE STANDS AT TIMES OF
CHALLENGE AND CONTROVERSY.
— Martin Luther King

623

Never run down the product of your
competitor—your customer won't
believe you anyhow!

624

Never speak ill of your competitors.

625

In a buyers' market the best is
still in the sellers' market.

7

Managing
Sales and Service

THE NEW PACKAGE LOOKS SO GOOD ON THE SHELVES THAT THE CUSTOMERS ARE LEAVING IT ON THE SHELVES

© Think Inc./Promod Batra

626

Life is short but there is always time for courtesy.

627

It ain't over, till it's over.

628

Lose one, gain two.

629

Tomorrow is another day.

630

Advertising makes promises; servicemen keep them.

631

Anyone can sell a one rupee item for 99 paisa.

632

The dog that trots about finds a bone.

633

They talk most who have least to say.

634

A man without a smiling face should not open a shop.

635

Being cheap is false economy.

636

Have a firm handshake.

637

Talk less, say more.

638

Visit your counterparts regularly.

639

Whatever the struggle, continue the climb; it may
be only one step to the summit.

640

Cut not the tree that gives you shade.

641

Selling a product is not an easy thing,
but the real test lies in selling yourself.

642

A sales-oriented accounts staff? Why not?

643

Quality of service before profit.

644

The best way to increase the sale of a product is
to improve the service.

645

Service is to sales like ink is to pen.
If the ink leaks in the best pen,
the pen is useless.

646

Stop worrying and start selling.

647

If your costs are going up, try lowering
your prices by selling more!

648

A difficult sale begins with the first call!

The manager relies on systems;
the leader relies on people.

649

Temper urgency with patience.

650

Many a "lost" sale has been saved by a final try.

651

Fool me once, shame on you; fool me twice,
shame on me.

652

What people say they will buy, they don't.

653

Courage at the critical moment is half the sale.

654

Many a sale has been won — or lost — in the
first three minutes.

655

A picture is equal to 1,000 words.
A visit is equal to 10,000 words.

656

A dissatisfied customer is like a spark
that can spread like wildfire.

657

A dissatisfied customer should not be taken
as an unwanted nuisance.

658

Out of the small orders of today grow the big
orders of tomorrow.

You don't have to be rich and wealthy to forgive and forget, but you have to be benevolent and have the maturity to think that way.

659

"Suppose we refund your money, send you
another part free of charge,
close the store and have the manager shot...
would that be satisfactory, sir?"

660

It is not the orders you hope to get, but the orders
you get that count.

661

If an order is hard to get, all the more glory goes
with getting it.

662

Please don't lose a customer for want of a part,
like the war was lost because of a nail.

663

Never forget, gentlemen, that we are salesmen—
not just demonstrators.

664

Any fact is better established by two or three good
testimonials than by a thousand arguments.

665

The dead are always content.

666

Selling is a noble profession because it
satisfies the needs of the buyer.
Just like a doctor cures a patient.

BECOME A TIGER SALESMAN!

The **"Pussy Cat Salesman"** does a fine job of prospecting and establishing the initial contact. He also makes a good presentation, but is not too sharp at replying to the sales objections. And when it comes to asking for the order, he becomes a docile pet. In his eagerness to be goody-goody, he loses sight of his main objective, that is bagging the order.

The **"Tiger Salesman"** is made of sterner stuff. He is nice to the prospect, but he is also firm. He is persistent and does not give up. In fact, he views every sales objection as an opportunity to tell more about his product. And finally, he does not hesitate to ask for it, that is, the customer's signature on the bottom line.

In the long run, tigers make more friends and close more sales too.

667

Selling may be applied common sense, but you will
need a good deal of training and
experience making practical use of it.

668

Close the sale, otherwise we are just wasting our time
and working for the competition.
Work systematically and ask for the order.

669

If there is any one secret of selling, it lies in the ability
to get the customer's point of view and see things
from his angle as well as from your own.

670

A sales call which is put off till tomorrow is
usually never made. Do it now!

671

Nothing will be sold if all possible objections
must first be overcome.

672

Writing memos to the boss about sales is
not the same as selling.

673

Be honest. If you don't know, say so.
If you know but won't tell, say so.

674

Good businessmen consider every lost order a disaster.
They learn from it and get prepared to
avoid another one.

675

Listening to a customer's complaint is 90% of the job;
taking necessary action is another 7%;
3% is following up with him to ensure satisfaction.

676

Good salesmen are problem-solvers.

677

The only way to get in the game is to
come out of the locker room.

678

Always think in terms of what the
other person wants.

679

If you have not sowed seed at the proper time,
you cannot reap at harvest time.

680

Adversity makes a salesman wise, not rich.

681

Agree, for the law is costly.

682

First think, and then speak.

683

More sales are lost through inability to express one's
thoughts and ideas than any other single cause.

684

Evaluate a lost sale.

Working together works.

There's no limit to what a man can do, as long as he doesn't mind who takes the credit. Team building works. Build a core group around yourself. American billionaire oil tycoon J. Paul Getty calls them "men with the millionaire mentality: people who are forward-thinking, cost-conscious and profit-oriented." And, they will build teams around themselves. It sure will become a pyramid reaching for the moon!

☐ Think Inc./Promod Batra

685

Negative salesmen are bad company.

686

No salesman ever says that he lost a customer
because of his faults!

687

Nothing ventured, nothing gained.

688

Once you open your mouth and start talking,
your customer starts dissecting you!

689

A salesman's trouble is not ignorance, but inaction.

690

Pick and choose the battles you fight; don't make
every problem a war.

691

Use field demonstration — as a closing tool.

692

Right is might, but no one wins who does not fight.

693

Rigidity and salesmanship do not go together.

694

Some salesmen forget they are salesmen
and try to be PR men.
Instead of sales, they seek admiration.

695

Silence is one great art of conversation.

WORKING TOGETHER WORKS

Even for our body to function well physically, it is very important that its parts work in perfect coordination. If any of the parts is damaged or becomes inactive, it has a crippling effect on the whole body. This is the simplest way to explain the concept of "Working Together Works."

In a machine, it is the various components of the mechanism that work together to make it run. The same is true for work situations where everybody must work together.

And, once you are working together, why not do it with a smile? Try asking for a favour from a colleague with your face all lit up. There is a remote possibility that he will refuse. A smile is like a drop of oil that makes the complex human mechanism work without friction. Spread a smile around and your workplace becomes a better place.

696

It takes Rs. 10,000 to get a customer.
It takes 10 seconds to lose one.
It takes 10 years for the problem to go away.

697

One person says, "Night has fallen,"
whereas another says, "Morning is coming!"

698

Opportunities may be missed,
but others will surely come your way.

699

Never falling is not an achievement.
Real achievement is rising again after a fall.

700

Speech is great, but silence is greater.

701

In the deepest water is the best fishing.

702

The more extensive a salesman's knowledge of
what has been done, the greater will be
his selling success.

703

Complaining about others is often
an admission of one's own incompetence.

704

The postage stamp secures succeeds because of
its ability to stick to one thing till it gets there.

TEAMWORK... BETTER FOR ALL

705

The great law which lies at the foundation of
all life is that our rewards in life will be
in exact proportion to our service.

706

The cause of failure lies within the salesman himself,
but he often seeks it in the customers.

707

Too many of us sell ourselves short.

708

Train your salesmen to talk to the customer in the
customer's language.

709

If a hunter opens fire at the shadow of an animal,
mistaking it for the animal itself,
he will finally have nothing left for himself
except empty cartridges.

710

Talent is only an enabler.
Competence is the engine that gets things done,
and it is developed only
through sweat, mistakes, bruises
and frustration.

711

When one door shuts, another opens.

712

Good after-sales service will increase
your market share.

PROFIT IS NOT A DIRTY WORD

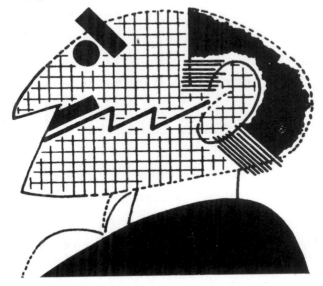

Profit is the driving force that spurs us on. It is the material yard-stick of success in business.

As long as you are not profiteering (that is, making money by unfair means), you need not feel guilty of making profit. It is your legitimate right, your means to growth, the incentive for you to give better products and service to the customer.

But putting profit before better quality and service is like putting the carriage before the horse—business does not move.

If, on the other hand, we strive for quality and service, our business goes galloping forward. And more profits come rolling in.

That's SUCCESS!

713

In a business, customers are normally underserviced.
Result: very slow growth.
Overservicing of customers means reduced profits.
Managing a business is the art of knowing the
difference between underservicing and overservicing.

714

Better quality is equal to fewer service problems.

715

Do not replace a part if repairing it can make it
almost as good as new. Do not repair a part if it
won't last. Tell this to your customers.

716

Have a sense of urgency when a customer comes
in for after-sales service.

717

It takes three years to get good results from
giving good service to customers.
Don't give up sooner.

718

Listen for more service when a
customer walks in.

719

Many businesses have succeeded without service
facilities, none without proper servicemen.

720

It is better to learn from the experience of others.

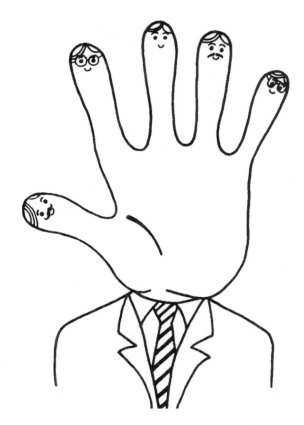

SALESMAN'S PERSISTENCE

A young salesman was finally admitted to the office of the president, who chided him, "Young man, you should feel flattered that I allowed you to come in here. I turned down five salesmen today."

"I know," replied the young salesman. "I was all five of them."

721

The greatest secret of all success is patience.
And the greatest secret of all failure is impatience.

722

The cost of after-sales service is so much
that quality assurance at every stage of
manufacturing proves to be cheaper
in the long run.

723

A business is like a game of tennis: the one who
serves well, seldom loses.

724

If you still have courage after
losing all, you can be rest assured
that you have not lost everything.

725

The sale really begins after the sale,
not before.

726

Your staff, unless you watch out,
will resort to every possible way to
underservice your customers.

727

Positive, repetitive self-talk changes our self-image.
And the suggestion we offer to ourselves
will be expressed in our actions.

728

Service is our success.

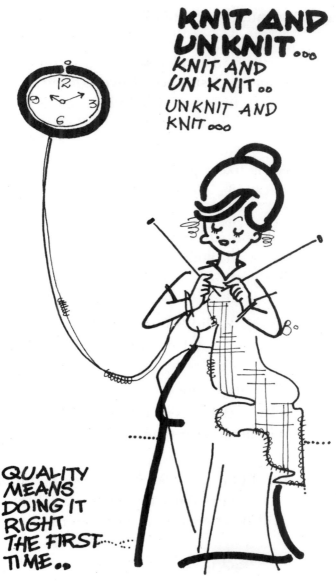

© Think Inc./Promod Batra

729

A good businessman sees his business
through a marketing eye as well as through
the general ledger.

730

A good manager always keeps the sand bucket
ready. And he keeps on looking for the smoke
from unlikely places.
Thus he is able to avoid devastating fires.

731

Don't allow the phone to interrupt important
moments. It's there for your convenience,
not the caller's.

732

We were collecting tons of statistics, but they did not
produce or sell cars.

733

A company and its dealers are partners.
Unless each one bothers about the other
half of the partnership, it doesn't
work for too long.

734

Look people in the eye.

735

A wall cannot be broken with just one push.
That way the wall remains standing,
but the head gets broken in the attempt.

736

Success follows patience;
too often people try to put them in the reverse order.

737

Refusing in a kind manner is better than making
promises which are not kept.

738

Find out what the customer wants and you may be in
for surprises. Many a time, he may want nothing.
Sometimes, he may simply want you to lend your
ear to his voice so that he can vent his feelings.

739

One should not remove the fly from
a friend's forehead with a hatchet.

740

Service, service, service... and more service.
While everybody wants it, most don't want to give it.

741

It is no use shaking the tree
when the leaves are still green.

742

Successful salesmanship is 90 per cent preparation
and 10 per cent presentation.

743

Wisdom is knowing when to speak your mind
and when to mind your speech.

If I don't go, I don't get...

There lived an old man with a rowboat who ferried passengers across a mile-wide river for ten paise.

Asked how many times a day he went back and forth, the old man said, "As many times as I can because the more I go, the more I get. And if I don't go, I don't get."

That's all you need to know—all there is to know—about business, economics, prosperity and self-respect.

744

Winners have a driving force that
keeps them winning.

745

Customers have an uncanny memory for keeping
track of who calls on them during good and less than
good times. Customers need service twelve months a
year. Don't get a reputation for being
a fair-weather salesman.

746

If your job is outside sales, stay outside.

747

Being organised is being motivated.

748

Be a consulting supplier, not an ordinary salesman.
Find answers for customers.

749

The unique thing about a winning attitude is that
it perpetuates itself.

750

Customers are influenced by your attitude.
Sales performance is built on sales attitude...
the desire to sell, the desire to get business.
And the aggressiveness to go after it.

751

Ask questions — carefully. Let the prospect talk.

752

Listen carefully, for selling clues and interests.

THE RATIO BETWEEN HARD WORK AND LUCK IS

Sow an action and reap a habit; sow a habit and reap a character; sow a character and reap a destiny.

Make hard work a daily habit, instead of lying supinely and waiting for a chance fruit to fall in your lap. Water the plant of fortune with drops of sweat. And see it grow and bear fruit!

Lady Luck smiles on those who have the will "to strike, to seek, to find and not to yield!" Miracles happen and the impossible becomes possible for those who work ceaselessly and never give up.

Know what you want! Work for it—and the earth will yield its treasures you!

753

Sell hard, to the prospect's interests, not your interests.

754

Develop answers to objections. Be ready.

755

Ask questions to get "yes" answers.

756

Practise presentations –– especially with new products,
new to you.

757

A man who has committed a mistake
and doesn't correct it
is committing another mistake.

758

Each employee contributes to customer satisfaction.

759

Selling is easy! It is the most
"commonsensical" of any profession.

760

A professional salesman, like a doctor or an engineer,
uses a variety of selling skills.

761

Product knowledge is only 20 to 30% of a
professional salesman's craft. The balance 70 to 80%
is divided between selling skills and attitude.

762

Selling techniques are almost the same,
whatever the product.

The harder we try, the luckier we are.

763

A positive selling attitude consists of
enthusiasm and confidence.

764

Salesmen normally do not listen.
They get a wrong notion that they must keep on
talking and talking, whether the prospect is listening
or not. Listen and hear what the prospect says.

765

Buyers will beat a path to your door...
provided you beat a path to their doors first.

766

Well done is better than well said.

767

However great the defeat is, it is always temporary.
With better planning the next time,
it can be converted into victory.

768

When the customer comes back for service,
I fight for him all the way to get him the best.
You've got to be like a doctor: something's wrong
with his car, so feel hurt for him.

769

In letter writing, 96 per cent is thinking and only
4 per cent is the actual writing.
A letter must contain a creative idea so that
the receiver can act on it and later remember
having taken action on it.

HEAR THE OTHER SIDE.

—*St. Augustine 334–430*

770

A sales letter is the most useful tool in
the kit of a sales manager, enabling him
to multiply his contacts with customers
and prospective customers a
thousand times.

771

Every letter that goes out on the company's
letterhead should be a sales letter. Either it
should sell goods cr it should sell goodwill.

772

A sales letter provides a means of contacting
and selling to customers in far-away places
where our salesman cannot call profitably.
In your area there are always some places
which are expensive to reach and it costs
too much to give an advertisement in local
papers; why not give a try to
good sales letters?

773

"I am sorry you have a problem, but I am glad
that you're bringing it to my attention.
It gives me a chance to help you."
Such simple statements have
done wonders.

774

Don't get into selling if you do not feel hurt
when your customer gets hurt.

SUCCESS
IS A JOURNEY, NOT A
DESTINATION.

Ensure that you are on the right road, moving
in the right direction—instead of
just at the right speed.

775

For every complaint received, the average company
has 24 customers who have had service problems,
six of which are considered serious.

776

Customers who have complained and have had their
complaints satisfactorily resolved will tell
an average of five other people about the favourable
treatment they received.

777

Even when a complaint isn't resolved in the
customer's favour, the fact that someone listened to
the complaint will greatly increase the likelihood of
return business.

8

Managing Marketing

"YOU MEAN IT'S TAKEN YOU THREE MONTHS TO FIND OUT THE TYPICAL CONSUMER IS UNDER TWENTY-ONE, WEARS WHISKERS AND PURRS!"

778

Marketing will not only sell good products;
it will also hasten the death of bad products.

779

Don't explain the features;
explain the benefits.

780

Expect the unexpected.

781

When the winds of change are blowing,
you need to know which way and how fast.

782

The pessimist complains about the wind;
the optimist expects it to change;
the realist adjusts the sails.

783

See it big, and keep it simple.

784

We do not always buy products;
we often buy images.

785

People don't buy things! They buy the benefits
that things provide.

786

Your image can never be stolen. Everything else can.

787

Changing conditions may cause a
monumental idea to become a tombstone.

197

Business is like riding a bicycle-either you keep moving or you fall down.

The name of the game is growth. You are either growing or going out of business! There is new business out there, no matter how depressed the market. All we have to do is to find out, and find out first. Concentrate your time, your brains and your resources on your successes. Bank your winners and abandon your losers.

788

It is often easier to get back the profits
than the market share.

789

Homilies: collect 1001 and your communication
skills will improve.

790

Selling is once. Marketing is when it is sold
again and again and again.

791

After learning the tricks of the trade, many of us think
we know the trade.

792

No one is so powerful that he can
harm others without harming himself.

793

No product, however good it may be, sells by itself.
That is where marketing comes in.

794

A good reputation is more valuable
than money.

795

Marketing is simply sales with
customer orientation.

796

Those who apply themselves too closely to little things
often become incapable of great things.

Statistics are often used as a drunkard uses a lamp post... not to light his way but to support his instability!

Someone once said: "There are three kinds of lies, viz. lies, damnable lies and statistics!" Whenever we collect business statistics, we must keep these words in mind. Collection of statistics costs a lot of money and time and if not done wisely, can mean money down the drain. But when collected using a bit of common sense, statistics can help in making better and faster decisions.

In some situations, the concept of approximation should be applied. An educated guess often may be cheaper and faster than collecting detailed information.

Statistics are no substitute for judgment. Most of us can recall the story about the statistician who, going by the average depth of a river, drowned in the middle.

797

This world is a world of competition.
If you do not get ahead of others,
they will get ahead of you.

798

Success does not make a company great;
what really matters is its contribution toward
making life better for everybody.

799

Don't forget the power of postcards.
Often that is all you need to get
the basic message across.

800

Business is never so healthy as when, like a chicken,
it must do a certain amount of
scratching for what it gets.

801

Concentration is the key to economic results...
no other principle of effectiveness is violated as
frequently today as the basic principle of
concentration...Our motto seems to be:
"Let's do a little bit of everything."

802

Think and do... one good deed per day for your
customer! When you are thinking and
doing you'll have no time to worry.
A good deed is one that brings a smile
of joy to the face of your customer.

UN CO-ORDINATED
REMEDIES FOR QUICK
OVERNIGHT RELIEF
WOULD EFFECT
ADVERSELY!!

803

What is the use of running when
we are on the wrong road?

804

Marketing is really a form of communication.

805

Beware of small expenses;
a small leak can sink a big ship.

806

Ninety per cent of punctures (flats) happen
in the last 10 per cent of tyre life.

807

A thoroughbred horse is not
dishonoured by its saddle.

808

Keep in touch with friends,
colleagues and books.

809

Learn to compromise. Learn to listen.

810

Look straight into the eyes of people,
employees and customers. Make it a habit.
It will give you more confidence.

811

It is better to make profit on
dirt than loss on muck.

312

If you have anxieties, go to sleep.

HAPPINESS IS A POSITIVE CASH FLOW

813

I will persist until I succeed.

814

Most speeches self-destruct within a day.
Make sure that yours is so good that it lasts for years.

815

Of all those arts in which the wise excel,
Nature's chief masterpiece is writing well.

816

Organisations learn and adapt v-e-r-y slowly.

817

People look for leadership in any get-together.
The essence of leadership is a point of view.
Never be afraid to have a point of view.
It is worth sixty IQ points.

818

Speak your mind once you have cultivated it well.
More often, your title is not relevant when you speak
from a well-furnished mind.

819

No seed turns into a tree by leaps and bounds.

820

The one who had the most information was the one
likely to get the most information in return.

821

The secret of success in conversation is to be able to
disagree without being disagreeable.

Those who foolishly sought power by riding on ~~the back of the tiger,~~ ended up inside.
— PRESIDENT JOHN F. KENNEDY

822

Even Napoleon lost one-third of all the
important battles he fought.

823

Selling well is doing certain things,
a certain way, every day.

824

The time to repair the roof is when
the sun is shining.

825

The best way to sell more is to
work more and loaf less.

826

Adhocism is the worst enemy of advertising.

827

If at first you don't succeed,
you're running about average.

828

When you say something, make sure you have said it.
The chances of your having said it are only fair.

829

No question is so difficult as that to
which the answer is obvious.

830

Gift wrap what you have to say or write.

831

Any fool can write a bad advertisement, but it takes a
genius to keep his hands off a good one.

The speed of the boss is the speed of the team.

Ralph Waldo Emerson rightly said: "An institution is the lengthened shadow of one man." History shows whenever a leader has achieved more than ordinary successes, he has gathered his team first. Of course, you have to inspire them, set course, provide the momentum and steer them in profitable directions.

© Think Inc./Promod Batra

832

Bad advertising can unsell a product.

833

Customers do not forgive bad quality,
untruthful advertising and being bored.

834

Don't expect your agency to pay for all
the dry holes they drill on your behalf.

835

It would be a swell world if everybody was as
pleasant as the fellow who's trying to sell you.

836

I sold three times. Not because the customers were
desperate to buy, but because I was desperate to sell.

837

Selling is an art: enthusiasm, innovativeness, and
ideas are some of the essential ingredients.

838

A satisfied customer is the best advertisement
for the product.

839

Frightened people are powerless to
produce good advertising.

840

Half the money you spend on advertising is wasted;
the trouble is you don't know which half.

841

Doing business without advertising is like
winking at a girl in the dark. You know what
you're doing, but nobody else does.

842

The best mental effort in the game of business is
concentrated on the major problem of securing the
consumer's rupee before the other person gets it.

843

There is new business out there, no matter
how depressed the market. All we have got to
do is to find it first. There are no prizes for
the seller who comes second.

844

He who has a product to sell and whispers
in a well is not going to get the rupees,
but he who climbs a tree and shouts will.

845

In selling, as in chess,
forethought wins.

846

Never give up a campaign just because you have
grown tired of it; customers don't see your
advertisements as often as you do.

847

Knowledge is power.

848

To convince others, you have to convince yourself.

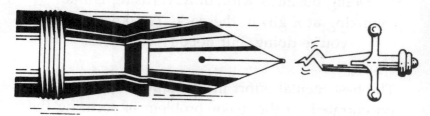

THE PEN IS MIGHTIER THAN THE SWORD

© Think Inc./Promod Batra

849

The computer is only yours faithfully and obediently.

850

Good communication can result in
the elimination of undesirable activities.

851

Take profit into account as late as you can;
take expenses into account as early as you can.

852

When you have written your headline,
you have spent eighty paise out of your rupee.

853

Anybody can cut prices, but it takes brains
to make a better product.

854

The fool says: "I have ruined my past
and my present." The wise man says:
"But the future is still safe."

855

Concentrate your time, your brains, and
your advertising money on your successes.
Bank your winners, and abandon your losers.

856

If your actions (or inaction)
have caused you to be left behind,
mere words will not push you ahead.

857

Follow the river and you'll go to the sea

COURAGE FACES FEAR AND THEREBY
MASTERS IT. COWARDICE REPRESSES
FEAR AND IS THEREBY MASTERED BY IT.
— Martin Luther King

858

Pretty cars sell. Ugly cars do not sell. It's simple.

859

If you are late in reaching the station,
you can't complain to the railways
that the train left without you.

860

Without competition, there is less
incentive to innovate.

861

New systems generate new problems.

862

Better cash management means better profits.

863

A big order can be lost by reaching late
for an appointment!

864

A 100-tractor dealership can be a losing proposition
while a 10-tractor dealership may be a big success.

865

Top management should spend 40 to 50 per cent of its
time educating and motivating its people.

866

Most people don't succeed in life because they don't
know what they want to achieve in the first place.

867

When business is good it pays to advertise;
when business is bad you've got to advertise

"the crow used stones to raise the level of water in the jug. LOOK AROUND, THINK AND SOLVE YOUR PROBLEMS WITH IMAGINATION.

216

868

While another person is talking, a polite silence is
golden, for it displays respect for the other's
intelligence and point of view.

869

Dress not to your liking, but to what you know or
think is the liking of the person you are meeting.

870

A blind man will not thank you for
a looking glass.

9

Managing Your Health & Happiness

Laughter is the best medicine. Learn to laugh at yourself, and tickle the funny-bone in others.

871
Greed is the heart's biggest enemy.

872
You must have goals,
but the goals should be achievable.

873
Moderation is advisable.

874
Don't save your good clothes; wear them.

875
Action kills the anxiety caused by procrastination.

876
Proper preparation prevents poor performance.

877
Take ups and downs with equanimity.

878
He that goes a borrowing, goes a sorrowing.

879
Most of the 'oohs' and 'aahs' are momentary.

880
Start a positive thoughts factory.
Good Ideas In and Good Ideas Out' — GIGO.

881
Look and think before you leap.

882
Change what you can and accept
what you cannot change.

When you reach for the stars, you may not quite get one, but you won't come up with a handful of dust either.

883

Insults and pills must not be chewed.

884

He who is slow to anger is better than the mighty.

885

God does not make faulty products.

886

When you try to spread happiness,
some of it sticks to you too!

887

If I give my word, no one can break it,
but if I sign this contract,
my lawyers can break it.

888

Don't expect gratitude from anyone,
including your wife!
Do whatever you can for the pleasure of doing
and giving to others.

889

The trick is to function with a level of stress that is
life enhancing, not life threatening.

890

Eating right will make you very old!

891

Don't carry your mistakes (and others' too)
in your heart for too long.

**Relax... even when your
wife shouts at you!**

892

If you are ten minutes early, you are already
late by five minutes. Plan to reach your work place
or an appointment early by fifteen minutes.

893

A smile is far better than the
most expensive Banarsi saree.

894

If you have to criticise, do it lovingly.

895

The faster you run, the less feedback you are able to
get and you distance yourself from the realities of
business. You end up making mistakes.

896

Accept sorrows and failures to enjoy happiness.

897

Agreements get better results than arguments.

898

Anger is an expensive luxury in which only men of a
certain income can indulge.

899

Many fears are born of fatigue and loneliness.

900

Crystals, carpets and chandeliers make a
nice house but only the smiles on the faces of the
residents make it a home!

901

Doing business should be a pleasure.

A man far too busy to care for his health is like a mechanic who is far too busy to care for his tools.

902

Health is happiness.

903

Think, thank and smile.

904

Never go to sleep with an argument unsettled.

905

Financial success is never having to balance
your cheque book.

906

Needs can be met, greeds never.

907

Anticipation breeds frustration.

908

He who lives content with little
possesses everything.

909

If sickness is unavoidable,
relax and enjoy it.

910

Laugh it off... a pressure cooker is no
good if it has no safety valve!

911

Be not merely good, be good for something.

912

Have a nice day.

WORK BANISHES THOSE THREE GREAT EVILS,
BOREDOM,
VICE
AND POVERTY.

—Voltaire

913

Think big thoughts...
but relish small pleasures.

914

Work is the best remedy for all ills.

915

Happy is he who is happy with his children.

916

You only live once but if you live right,
once is enough.

917

Praise is the best diet for us, after all.

918

The most manifest sign of wisdom is
continued cheerfulness.

919

Angels fly, it is said, because they
take themselves lightly.

920

Businessmen who do not know how to
fight worry die young.

921

To love oneself is the beginning of a
lifelong romance.

922

A good day's work begins with a
good night's rest.

You cannot be anything if you want to be everything.

923

It is riches of the mind only
that make a man rich and happy.

924

The smallest good deed is better than
the grandest good intention.

925

A wise man is one who asks for more,
but is willing to take less.

926

Always have something beautiful in sight,
even if it's just a daisy in a jelly glass.

927

Fortunately, happiness is something that
depends not on position but on disposition.

928

The growth of wisdom can be accurately
gauged by the drop in ill temper.

929

Have a golden tongue and a golden pen.

930

Ninety-one per cent of financial worries are
a result of 3 per cent each of carelessness,
laziness and overspending.

931

If you look for the positive things in life.
you'll find them.

932

Flattery is counterfeit, and like counterfeit money,
it will eventually get you into
trouble if you try to pass it.

933

When we have accepted the worst, we have nothing
more to lose. Result: true peace of mind.

934

To kill stress, now or in the future, you need
enthusiasm and creativity.

935

Do not grieve over hardship.
Hardship makes the man.

936

The mind in its own place and in itself can make a
heaven of hell, a hell of heaven.

937

Build your "memory bank" now before it is
too late to make deposits.

938

If we want to find happiness, let s stop thinking about
gratitude or ingratitude and give for
the inner joy of giving.

939

I wasn't interested in making a lot of
money, but I was interested in
making a good living.

IF YOU WANT HAPPINESS FOR A DAY...
GO ON A PICNIC.

940

Be large of heart and succeed.
Be small of heart and fail.

941

Change yourself and your life will change on its own.

942

Ten poor men can sleep comfortably under
one blanket, while two kings cannot be
contained in one kingdom.

943

It is difficult to worry while you are busy doing
something that requires planning and thinking.

944

You can choose to get drunk tonight —
but when you do, you have also
chosen to feel miserable tomorrow.

945

Everybody in the world is seeking happiness —
and there is one sure way to find it.
That is by controlling your thoughts.

946

Worry is like the constant drip, drip of water;
and the constant drip, drip, drip of worry often
drives men to insanity and suicide.

947

Contentment is a pearl of great price.
Whoever procures it at the expense of ten thousand
desires makes a wise and happy purchase.

IF YOU WANT HAPPINESS FOR A WEEK...
GO ON A VACATION.

948

Think and thank. Think of all we have to be grateful
for, and thank God for all our boons and bounties.

949

Yes, you are wealthy. But I am rich.

950

Don't fuss about trifles. Don't permit little
things to ruin your happiness.

951

The greatest mistake physicians make is that they
attempt to cure the body without attempting to cure
the mind, yet the mind and body are one and
should not be treated separately.

952

When fate hands us a lemon, let's try to make a
lemonade. Do the very best you can: and then put up
your old umbrella and keep the rain of criticism from
running down the back of your neck.

953

If you can't sleep, get up and work or read until
you do feel sleepy. Remember that no one was ever
killed by lack of sleep. Worrying about insomnia
usually causes far more damage than
sleeplessness. Try prayer.

954

Happiness is a perfume which you cannot pour on
others unless you have some on you.

IF YOU WANT HAPPINESS FOR A MONTH...
GET MARRIED.

955

Happiness is achievement. Achievement of goals.
Goals of helping someone, doing it yourself,
and thinking good thoughts. Happiness is doing.

956

You cannot prevent the birds of sadness from
flying over your head, but you can prevent
them from nesting in your hair.

957

When you feel good about yourself,
you improve your self-image, and
it is a fact that that reduces your stress.

958

Looking for happiness is like clutching a shadow
or chasing the wind.

959

Even Alexander the Great was carried to the
burial ground with two empty palms
showing outside his shroud. Think... give away
what you cannot use in your lifetime.

960

Thanks can come from the head or the heart.
The ones from the heart are warmer; they
are appreciated and remembered.

961

Happiness is not having what you want but
wanting what you have.

IF YOU WANT HAPPINESS FOR A YEAR
... INHERIT WEALTH.

962

Give to the world the best you have and
the best will come back to you.

963

Some people worry because they do not have
anything to worry about!

964

If we think happy thoughts, we will be happy.
If we think miserable thoughts, we will be miserable.
If we think fear thoughts, we will be fearful.

965

Allowing emotion to govern one's actions brings
failure. Acting with restraint brings success.

966

Happiness results from discipline.
A regular life is very essential for happiness.

967

Nature gave you your face,
but you have to provide the expression.

968

Happy memories require preparation.

969

Getters generally don't get happiness; givers do.

970

If you are patient in one moment of anger,
you will escape a hundred days of sorrow.

IF YOU WANT HAPPINESS FOR A LIFETIME...
LEARN TO LOVE WHAT YOU DO.

971

What the mind of a man can conceive, and believe,
it can achieve. Conceive HAPPINESS.

972

One should be honest and
also appear to be honest.

973

One small deed accomplishes more than
a thousand words.

974

Some of our problems are self-inflicted.

975

Staying calm is the best way to take the
wind out of an angry person's sails.

976

Practise abstinence, for riches will not last

977

Take time off to make yourself happy.
Use your "third eye" to see what makes you happy.

978

The only goal which is common
to all mankind is to attain happiness.

979

The happiness of your life depends on the
wholesomeness of your thoughts.

980

The secret of happiness is curiosity.

SUCCESS HAS A SIMPLE FORMULA:
DO YOUR BEST, AND PEOPLE MAY LIKE IT.

981

Think and act cheerfully and
you will feel cheerful.

982

A wise man is one who can live in peace
with things he cannot change.

983

We can give others happiness only if we ourselves
are sufficiently happy.

984

Good attitudes do not result from good positions
or wealth. The fact is that people get good positions
because of their positive attitudes.

985

Worry often gives a small thing a big shadow.

986

Worrying is a function of the idle mind.

987

Men leave home because their wives nag.

988

May every day of the coming year add to your
prosperity, subtract your worries, multiply your
happiness, and divide your problems with equal
number of solutions!

989

Don't worry, be happy.

990

Walk straight in your life.

Laugh, and even the birds laugh with you. "Laughter is prayer. If you can laugh, you have learnt how to pray. Don't be serious. Only a person who can laugh, not only at others but at himself also, can be religious."

— *Osho Rajneesh*

991

Don't ever look for shortcuts or compromise
with your conscience.

992

Are you getting 'smileage' from your business?

993

Healthy people think of themselves.
Sick people neglect themselves.

994

An honest day's work is the best medicine for all ills.

995

People who cannot find time for recreation are
obliged sooner or later to find time for illness.

996

A milligram of prevention saves tonnes of cure.

997

Success depends upon outlook.

998

Good deeds cut off tongues.

999

Bring your hearts together, but keep your
tents separate.

1000

Keep physically fit, mentally alert and
spiritually strong.

1001

The only happy man is he who thinks he is.

Problems, problems everywhere...

What's wrong with having problems? The only people who have no problems are in cemeteries. Problems are a sign of life. So be glad you've got them. It means you are alive. The more problems you have, the more alive you are. If you have no problems, better get down on your knees and ask: "Lord, don't you trust me anymore? Give me some problems."

1002

Pray about every difficult problem.

1003

Think objectively and keep a sense of humour.
Make the business fun for you and others.

1004

Failure is only the opportunity to begin again
more intelligently.

1005

There is no disgrace in honest failure;
there is disgrace in fearing to fail.

1006

A sharp dagger only wounds the flesh,
but a sharp tongue can wound the spirit.

1007

My life has been full of terrible misfortunes,
most of which never happened.

1008

Some people know how to live everyone's
life but their own.

1009

Three and 3 can make 33 and zero as well as 6!
Therefore, THINK and use your imagination.

1010

Many a wife has made her own marital grave with a
series of little digs.

HAPPINESS IS NEVER
PERFECT UNLESS
IT IS SHARED..

1011

There are two types of pleasures: simple pleasures
make you stressfree, while foolish pleasures
make you stressful.

1012

Ninety per cent of the things in our lives are
right and 10 per cent are wrong.

1013

When your neighbour's house is on fire,
your own property is at stake.

1014

Happiness doesn't depend on outward conditions,
it depends on inner conditions.

1015

I had the blues because I had no shoes, until upon
the street, I met a man who had no feet.

1016

We do not smile because we are happy;
we are happy because we smile.

1017

Two men looked out from prison bars;
one saw the mud, the other saw stars.

1018

I believe in work, for discontent and
labour are not often companions.

1019

Time is always passing,
and it never returns.

When you look at him, what do you feel? Well, I start laughing inside! Why? Because he was an honest and innocent person who always got into innocent troubles. If you want to kill your stress, see his films. Think of similar people, places, and incidents which make you laugh.

1020

A good secret of how best to use each day's time
is to try to pack it like a suitcase, filling up the small
spaces with small things.

1021

Try to complete the least urgent in the time you
have allowed yourself because left-over tasks
steal part of tomorrow's time.

1022

A mean father has thieves for children.

1023

Happiness lies, first of all, in health.

1024

Man is the only creature endowed
with the power of laughter.

1025

A good laugh is like sunshine in a house.

10

Managing Your Thoughts

*DESCARTES

Man's ability to think distinguishes him from the animals.

1026
Birds drink from a tank,
but they cannot empty it.

1027
Experience teaches you to first get all your pertinent
data together and, second, to analyse it properly.
The first requires discipline; the second,
years of experience.

1028
Indecision is often worse than a wrong decision.

1029
Unlike the overuse to which our livers, hearts, lungs
and mouths are subjected, our brains are seldom
called upon to perform anything even close
to their capacities.

1030
Overplanning... look for it and kill it.

1031
Think the unthinkable!

1032
Success needs no explanation;
failure has none.

1033
Never fear shadows; they simply mean that there
is a light shining somewhere nearby.

1034
You can't do things differently until
you see things differently.

Then what...?

Henry Ford bought flowers for his wife from a shop every Friday evening. Once, he asked the old florist, "Gentleman, you have a good shop. Why not open a branch?" Florist, "Sir, then what?" Henry Ford, "You will then have several branches in Detroit." Florist, "Sir, then what?" Henry Ford, "Then all over the USA." Florist, "Sir, then what?" Henry Ford, angrily, "Damn it, you will then be able to relax." Florist, "That is what I am doing even now." Ford walked away sheepishly.

1035

Your mind is a Bank Account. Deposit good ideas,
positive thoughts and pleasant experiences in it.
For example, refuse to view sub-standard TV or
video programmes. Result? You can withdraw...
good ideas.

1036

Your mind is a computer and,
therefore, programmable.

1037

Your mind is a Thoughts Factory, and you are the
production manager. It can produce either positive or
negative thoughts. The ideas of others are your
raw materials.

1038

Fight for the kings, queens and bishops, but throw
away the pawns. A habit of graceful surrender on
trivial issues will make you difficult to resist when
you stand and fight on a major issue.

1039

Listen to others but use your own judgment.

1040

Mistakes are the best teachers.

1041

A hunch is creativity trying to tell you something.

1042

Never pay a compliment as if you
expected a receipt.

GETTING IDEAS
IS LIKE SHAVING —

IF YOU DON'T DO IT
EVERYDAY, YOU'RE A BUM.

1043

A lightning call is the result of a post card not having
been mailed when it should have been...

1044

Ninety-six per cent of the old records and
letters are never referred to again.

1045

Banks are just like any business.
They are out to make profits.
Do not put all your business in one bank.

1046

A grain of sand or a grain of wheat contains more
knowledge than a library; all we have to do is to ask,
ask and ask.

1047

One man with courage can make a majority.

1048

Creativity is not a function of size. Small is beautiful.
A smart chartered accountant may be more effective
than the biggest accounting firm.

1049

Don't be afraid of your auditors.
Massage their egos and they will
help you to improve your profits by
telling you about avoidable activities.

1050

Before you kick the dog,
find out the name of its master.

Keep your mind 6-9% empty...

An American professor goes to a Zen master to learn about Zen Buddhism. The Zen master pours tea in a cup for the professor. After some time, it starts spilling and the professor shouts, "Stop, no more will go in the cup." The Zen master replies, "Likewise, your mind is full of your own ideas. How can I teach you Zen till you empty your mind to learn about it?" THINK. Keep your minds 6% to 9% empty for new ideas to flow in.

1051

Not even the most productive cow can be milked
forever without investment.

1052

Be patient while analysing and impatient
while executing.

1053

The best photograph in the world is no good if it is
still in somebody's camera.

1054

The first mistake a great many people make in
their financial planning is to think of their
salaries in total, before income tax has been
deducted. A cardinal rule is to erase
the gross salary from your mind and
concentrate only on your net salary.

1055

Too many people care more about always doing things
the right way, rather than doing the right thing.

1056

A good manager is one who gets the maximum from
his equipment. A better manager is one who gets
the maximum from business. An even better manager
is one who manages his business. And a far better
manager is one who plants seeds of thinking
in the minds of his men.

1057

A company is a long shadow of the boss.

"DON'T WORRY
OVER WHAT OTHER
PEOPLE ARE THINKING
ABOUT YOU. THEY ARE
BUSY WORRYING OVER
WHAT YOU ARE THINKING
ABOUT THEM ..."

1058

A person who uses his imagination creatively may do better than a person with more resources of men, money and materials.

1059

Build houses.
Don't build blunders.

1060

Business is a "get-things-done" situation.

1061

Busy people don't like to spend five minutes for something that should take one.

1062

Get rid of grey thinking every night while you are trying to sleep.

1063

Hundreds of businessmen have succeeded without an M.B.A. but none without common sense.

1064

Knowledge and good manners are equally essential for success in business.

1065

Management attracts capital, and capital attracts men. It cannot be done any other way.

1066

Managers can look good on the bottom line but at the same time may be destroying the company by failing to invest in the future.

LIBERTY
IS THE ONLY THING
YOU CANNOT HAVE
UNLESS
YOU ARE WILLING TO
GIVE IT TO OTHERS.

1067

Managers do things the right way.
Leaders do the right things.

1068

Many companies do not have exit gates for ideas,
paper, people, products.

1069

Many people have lost their businesses
because they expanded.

1070

Minefields of the business world:
anger, jealousy, revenge.

1071

You must first clearly see a thing in your mind
before you can do it.

1072

Profit is important, but you must invest to build up
assets which you can cash in in the future.

1073

The most successful executive is not necessarily the
individual who is the most original, but the person
who can add to original knowledge by using the
successful ideas of others.

1074

The only difference between a good manager and
a so-so manager is that one makes a decision
in 30 seconds while the other makes
the same decision in 30 days.

For every 10 minutes you are angry,
you lose 600 seconds of happiness!

1075

Never lose your curiosity.
It is what keeps your mind agile.

1076

What are you doing today to be
in business tomorrow?

1077

You cannot be successful in any business without
believing that it is the greatest business in the world.
You have to put your heart into the business and the
business into your heart.

1078

A simple match-stick is a portable and pocketable fire.
But, imagine life without it.

1079

A two-word success story: Work works.

1080

All too often people believe that creativity
automatically leads to innovation.

1081

Always be a front seater.
You will start feeling bigger and smarter.

1082

Ask and you shall receive;
demand and you will get less.

1083

Bad news always flies faster than good.

Are you like the proverbial blind men who look at things in parts (what you like to see or do), or do you look at things as a whole (to see all and to do what is to be done)?

1084

Between saying and doing one often wears out
a good pair of shoes.

1085

By silence, I hear other men's imperfections
and conceal my own.

1086

Chop your own wood and it will warm you twice.

1087

Clothes don't make a person,
but they speak for you.

1088

Computers will not make bad business good.

1089

Creativity is thinking up new things;
innovation is doing new things.
There is no shortage of creativity or creative
people; the shortage is of innovators.

1090

Direction is more important than speed.
We are so busy looking at our speedometers
that we forget the milestone.

1091

Entrepreneurs are people with great imagination.

1092

Don't destroy your spirit for
"this quarter" or "this year" gains.

George Reeves was a huge man, 6 feet 2 inches, weighing seventeen stone. He was my teacher in the fifth grade. In class, he would suddenly shout, "Silence." Then he would print in big letters on the blackboard the word CAN'T. Turning to the class, he would demand, "And now what shall I do?" Knowing what he wanted, we chanted back, "Knock the T off the CAN'T." With a sweeping gesture, he would erase it, leaving the word CAN. Dusting the chalk from his fingers, he would say, "Let that be a lesson to you—you can if you think you can."

1093

Don't change with the change;
change before the change.

1094

He who opens a school closes a prison.

1095

I regret often that I have spoken;
never that I have been silent.

1096

Ideas are useless unless used.

1097

If someone pelts you with stones,
do not quarrel with him. Try rather to
raise yourself to such a height that
the stones cannot reach you.

1098

If you want peace, you must
prepare for war.

1099

Is he a big man or a great man?
The lowliest of persons may be a
great man and the biggest may turn
out to be the smallest.

1100

It is a good thing that God does not let you
look into the future: otherwise you may be
tempted to shoot yourself.

TAKE TIME TO THINK, IT HELPS..
DONT JUST REACT..

1101

It is a funny thing about life; if you refuse to accept
anything but the best, you very often get it.

1102

It is easy to give money to those who have talent,
but almost impossible to give talent to
those who have money.

1103

It is the first step that is difficult.

1104

Knowledge and timber shouldn't be much
used till they are seasoned.

1105

Little thieves are hanged,
but great ones escape.

1106

Live in the present, and make it so beautiful that it
will be worth remembering.

1107

Long runners can't be short runners.

1108

Many of us have secure cabins on sinking ships.

1109

Most of us have a weakness for self-depreciation.
Watch out!

1110

My shopping was shopping for knowledge.

We should think over what we have read, digest it and make it an integral part of our daily life.

—MAHATMA GANDHI

1111

Never bet more on a sure thing than
you can afford to lose.

1112

Never break a person's rice bowl or
let him lose his face.

1113

Never explain your troubles to anyone. No one is
interested in wasting time to hear your troubles.

1114

No one can ever insult you when you
know your own worth.

1115

Shooting fish in a barrel may not be sporting. But if
the purpose is to get fish, it works.

1116

Oil is lubrication between machine parts,
but creates friction among nations.

1117

When a little voice inside says "no", don't bully it.

1118

In the long run, everyone has to die.

1119

Smile big ! A big smile gives you confidence

1120

The higher the monkey climbs the more
he shows his tail.

1121

The day you get the big idea is the day to
begin to improve that idea.

1122

The higher a man goes, the narrower his thinking
becomes. Therefore, watch out.

1123

The banker is the only person I know
selling something everybody wants.

1124

The greater the storm, the sooner it's over.

1125

To endure the unendurable makes a child into a man.

1126

To make a one pound comb of honey,
bees must collect nectar from about
two million flowers.

1127

Too much of the world is run on the theory
that you don't need road manners
if you are a five tonne truck.

1128

We are often our own worst enemy.

1129

When our small children hit a table,
we blame the table!
Wrong training.

LOVE, TRUTH, AND THE COURAGE TO DO WHAT
IS RIGHT SHOULD BE OUR OWN GUIDEPOSTS
ON THIS LIFELONG JOURNEY.
— Coretta Scott King

1130

When you are number 2 or 3, try harder.
And when you are number 1, try even harder.

1131

When you get to the end of your rope,
tie a knot and hang on.

1132

A man is not finished when he is defeated;
he is finished when he quits.

1133

Whenever a man falls, it is usually at the point where
he thinks he is strong.

1134

Wisdom lies not in the amount of knowledge acquired
but in the degree of its application.

1135

You may be right in the short term, but in the long
run it may amount to a blunder!

1136

You must learn to accept defeat without being
defeated.

1137

You never know what you can do till you try.

1138

You never miss the water till the well runs dry.

1139

Learn from the past to improve the future.

THINK

there must be a better way!

Your brain is a power-house of creative energy.

From this amazing thinking-machine spring bold new ideas. Ideas that can work rare miracles. Like the ideas that have moved man from the first wheel to the supersonic jet.

Think! Unleash your creative power. And you will make astounding discoveries. Thomas Edison tried ten thousand times to develop an incandescent lamp and failed ten thousand times. But he kept searching for a better way of doing it and finally invented the electric bulb.

You too can do your miracles of the mind. And find better ways of bettering life.

1140

If the camel hadn't knelt down,
it couldn't have been loaded.

1141

Your name is your trademark.
Protect it as if it is your life.

1142

The difference between you and me is only one of
hearing; where you hear a door close, I hear it open.

1143

There is no rose without thorns, but one who
broods on the existence of thorns without
giving any thought to the beauty of the roses
above them is like the man who looks
at mud in preference to the stars.

1144

The most wasted day of all is that on which
you have not laughed.

1145

To an executive his company is his mistress.

1146

No tree has ever reached the sky.

1147

The loaded gun terrifies one man;
the unloaded gun terrifies two.

1148

In every house there is a drain.

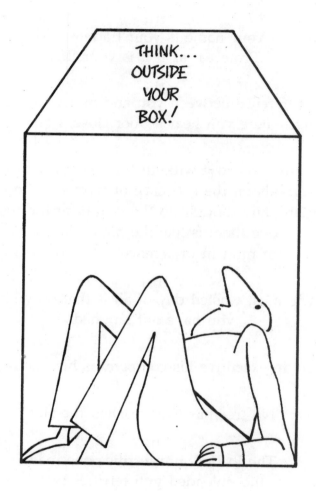

1149

Every obnoxious act is a cry for help.

1150

If you have a sore the flies will find it.

1151

All things are difficult before they become easy.

1152

Do not suppose a man can cook just because you
see him blowing on the fire.

1153

Colours fade, temples crumble, empires fall...
but wise words endure.

1154

When you reach forty, you suffer from a new
ailment every year.

1155

If you really want to annoy your enemy,
keep silent and leave him alone.

1156

We are vessels of varying size;
success is not how large but how full.

1157

Gauge a person not by how much they need in life,
but how little.

1158

It feels so good to be good.

Nothing dies faster than a new idea in a closed mind.

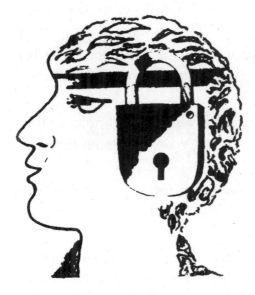

In the history of mankind, whenever man has opened the shutters of his mind, healthy new ideas have breezed in. And he has vigorously stepped out of his narrow confines to discover continents and oceans, planets and galaxies.

But whenever man has shut out new ideas and gone into hibernation in the safety of old, rigid norms, human civilization has been shrouded by the gloom of a Dark Ages.

Now shake yourself out of your slumber. Step out of the den of stagnant thoughts, into the open field of bold new ideas. Soar high on the strength of an exploring mind to reach unknown heights of achievement and success.

1159

Apologise quickly and graciously —
anger slowly and thoughtfully.

1160

Until we forgive, we ferment.

1161

Write your injuries in sand and
your advantages in marble.

1162

Believe half of what you see and
none of what you hear.

1163

The barn has burnt down but now I can see the sea.

1164

Wealth Lost — Something Lost.
Honour Lost — Much Lost.
Courage Lost — All Lost !

1165

The man who makes no mistakes does
not usually make anything.

1166

A day to come seems longer than a year that's gone.

1157

Generosity should be digestible.

1168

You are as good as your last surgery or last sale or
whatever else you do.

Compare Akbar the Great and the pragmatist Aurangzeb. While Akbar was ahead of his time by nearly three centuries, Aurangzeb trailed behind his age by at least half as many hundred years. Akbar, a lover of books, mostly through his Navratnas, focussed on the essentials of his job and was stressfree throughout his rule. Aurangzeb was always stressful, and the opening line of his will was, "I was helpless in life and I am departing helpless." Read a book on Akbar the Great to be stressfree.

1169

Keep your sense of humour intact.
It helps fight tension.

1170

If you have too many jobs to do at once,
sit back and pick the three most important ones.

1171

Don't neglect your hobbies and you
will find that you are more creative.

1172

My mind and my heart are my best assets.
I must "invent" them, consciously and
subconsciously, through exposure and experience —
every day, before I go to sleep.

1173

Discovery consists of looking at the same
thing as everyone else and thinking
something different.

1174

One of the greatest strengths God has given
to a human being is the ability to forget.

1175

To prejudge is to be prejudiced.

1176

Success without honour
is like food without salt...
it will satisfy your hunger,
but it won't taste good.

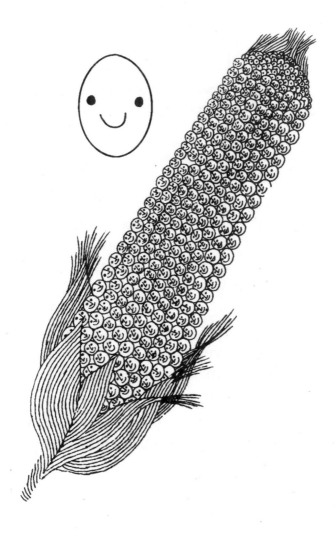

Your mind is like an acre of land. You have to sow it (with ideas), till it (with readings), fertilize it (with visits to counterparts), and apply pesticides (to prevent it from becoming inanimate) to get the best crop of results.

1177

No point in taking three weeks to make a decision
that can be made in three seconds and corrected
inexpensively later if wrong. The whole organisation
may be out of business while you
oscillate between baby-blue or
buffalo-brown coffee cups.

1178

A short pencil is better than a long memory.

1179

It isn't that they can't see the solution;
it's that they can't see the problem.

1180

It is not the weather cock that changes;
it is the wind.

1181

You can't get an "A" if you don't do your homework.

1182

Second thoughts are ever wiser.

1183

It takes only one or two insensitive employees to
convince a person that he's dealing with an
impersonal monolithic giant.

1184

Life is easier when you do things right the first time.
As they say, "When you hit a home run
you can take your time running the bases."

Look deep inside, things are seldom what they seem.

1185

Excellence means doing the little things well — doing
a thousand things one per cent better rather than
doing one thing a thousand per cent better.

1186

Improvements are sold by the inch
rather than by the yard.

1187

Excellence means caring; it means making a
special effort to do more.

1188

Blessed is he who has found his work;
let him ask for no other blessing.

1189

No one can make you feel inferior
without your consent.

1190

Don't undertip the waiter just because the
food is bad, he didn't cook it.

1191

About the only thing that comes to us without
effort is old age.

1192

Besides the noble art of getting things done,
there is the noble art of leaving things undone.
The wisdom of life consists in the
elimination of non-essentials.

1193

Most people wish to serve God —
but in an advisory capacity only.

1194

The game of life is a game of boomerangs
Our thoughts, deeds and words return to us
sooner or later with astounding accuracy.

1195

Luck is what happens when
preparation meets opportunity.

1196

We ought to be able to learn some things secondhand.
There is not enough time for us to make all
the mistakes ourselves.

1197

Success has no rules. but you can learn a great
deal from failure.

1198

To keep a lamp burning we have to
keep putting oil in it.

1199

The trouble with the rat race is that even if you win,
you're still a rat.

1200

The only difference between a rut and
a grave is their dimensions.

Why Worry?

There are only two things to worry about.
Either you are well or you are sick.
If you are well, then there is nothing to worry about.
But if you are sick there are only two things to worry about;
Whether you will get well, or whether you will die.
If you get well, there is nothing to worry about;
But if you die, there are only two things to worry about:
Whether you go to heaven or hell.
If you go to heaven there is nothing to worry about;
And if you go to hell you'll be so busy shaking hands with old friends,
You won't have time to worry.
SO WHY WORRY!

1201

It has always been and always will be the same in the
world: The horse does the work and the
coachman is tipped.

1202

The climb out of that rut can look
like the highest mountain.

1203

It is not enough to have a good mind;
the main thing is to use it well.

1204

The bigger the organisation, the longer it
takes to get a little job done.

1205

Pride is the mask of one's own faults.

1206

Those who play with cats must
expect to be scratched.

1207

You cannot drive straight on a twisting lane.

1208

A bad cause requires many words.

1209

Nearly all men can stand adversity,
but if you want to test a man's character,
give him power.

YOU OUGHT TO BELIEVE SOMETHING
IN LIFE, BELIEVE THAT THING SO
FERVENTLY THAT YOU WILL STAND UP
WITH IT TILL THE END OF YOUR DAYS...
WE HAVE A POWER, A POWER AS OLD AS
THE INSIGHTS OF JESUS OF NAZARETH AND
AS MODERN AS THE TECHNIQUES OF
MAHATMA GANDHI.
—Martin Luther King

1210

Management is now where the medical profession was
when it decided that working in a drug store was not
sufficient training to become a doctor.

1211

If two men on the same job agree all the time,
then one is useless. If they disagree all the time,
then both are useless.

1212

You will benefit in the long run if you give
credit down the line for ideas that
originated in your own mind.

1213

Never fight with a man who has nothing to lose.

1214

The surest way for an executive to kill
himself is to refuse to learn how, and when,
and to whom to delegate work.

1215

What is worth doing is worth the trouble of asking
somebody else to do.

1216

I would suggest that the B.A. degree be issued
on paper which deteriorates in five years.

1217

There is nothing so useless as doing efficiently that
which should not be done at all.

Choose happiness...

An old man appeared on a popular television programme. He had received a prize for having won a contest. He stole the show with his exuberant spirit and quick wit. "It's easy to see," remarked the admiring master of ceremonies, "that you are a very happy man. What's the secret of being as happy as you are? Let us zero in on it." "Why, son," the old man answered, "it's as plain as the nose on your face. When I wake up in the morning, I have two choices. One is to be unhappy. And I want you to know, son, that I'm not as dumb as I may look. I'm smart enough to choose happiness. I just make up my mind to be happy. . . that's all there is to it."

1218

Don't put off for tomorrow what you can do today,
because if you enjoy it today you can do it
again tomorrow.

1219

One of the greatest labour-saving inventions
of today is tomorrow.

1220

The harder you work, the luckier you get.

1221

It is not half as important to burn the midnight oil
as it is to be awake in the daytime.

1222

If people always did naturally what was best for the
enterprise, then there would be no need for
administration.

1223

Being powerful is like being a lady. If you have to
tell people you are, you ain't.

1224

Grow antennae, not horns.

1225

A nose that can see is worth two that can sniff.

1226

Never claim as a right what you can ask as a favour.

1227

A little uncertainty is good for everyone.

If you are unhappy...

Once upon a time, there was a non-conforming sparrow who decided not to fly south for the winter.

However, soon the weather turned so cold that he reluctantly started to fly south. In a short time ice began to form on his wings and he fell to earth in a farmyard, almost frozen to death.

A cow passed by and shat on the little sparrow. The sparrow thought it was the end. But the manure warmed him and defrosted his wings. Warm and happy, able to breathe, he started to sing. Just then a large cat came by and hearing the chirping, investigated the sounds.

The cat cleared away the manure, found the chirping bird and promptly ate him.

The moral of the story is:

1. Everyone who shits on you is not necessarily your enemy.
2. Everyone who gets you out of the shit is not necessarily your friend.
3. And if you're warm and happy in a pile of shit, keep your mouth shut.

1228

All work and no play makes Ram's wife
a wealthy widow.

1229

In telephoning for a taxi to meet a
specific engagement, such as a train
or a dinner, it is better to ask that
the taxi call at 6:55 rather than at 7 p.m.
An even hour is vague,
but an odd hour is specific.

1230

You must have long-range goals to keep from being
frustrated by short-range failures.

1231

If you have always done it that way,
it is probably wrong.

1232

The most common source of mistakes in management
decisions is the emphasis on finding the right answer
rather than the right question.

1233

The best labour-saving device is a wastebasket,
i.e. file no. 13.

1234

The busiest men have the fullest wastebaskets.

1235

The occupational disease of a poor executive is
the inability to listen.

Abraham Lincoln became President of the U.S.A when he was 51 after a string of failures. Because he was a good president, people criticised him the most. To remain stressfree, his thinking was crystal clear: No man is good enough to be president, but someone has to be!

1236

A compromise is the art of dividing a cake in such a
way that everyone believes he has the biggest piece.

1237

When one divides, the other should have
the right of first choice.

1238

A word of advice: don't give it!

1239

Once a man would spend a week patiently waiting if
he missed a stage coach, but now he rages if he misses
the first section of a revolving door.

1240

The other line always moves faster.

1241

When the man you like switches from what he said a
year ago, or four years ago, he is a broadminded
person who has courage enough to change his mind
with changing conditions. When a man you don't like
does it, he is a liar who has broken his promise.

1242

Hard work coupled with common sense spells success.

1243

Our attitude determines our altitude.

1244

Those who don't read good books have no advantage
over those who can't.

Two boys were walking down a country road when they saw two milk cans being loaded for delivery in a nearby city. Seeing no one, the boys lifted off the cover of Can Number 1 and dropped in a big bullfrog. Then they lifted off the cover of Can Number 2 and dropped in another bullfrog. Later the cans were picked up and loaded for city delivery.

During the journey, the bullfrog in Can Number 1 said: "This is terrible! I can't lift off the cover of the can because it's too heavy. I have never had a milk bath before, and I can't reach to the bottom of the can to get enough push to lift the cover, so, what's the use" — and he gave up trying and quit! When the cover of Can Number 1 was taken off, there was a big dead bullfrog.

The same conditions existed in Can Number 2 and the frog said to himself: "Well, I can't lift off the cover because it's too tight and too heavy. I haven't got a brace and bit to drill a hole to save myself, but, by the great Father Neptune, there is one thing I learned to do in liquids and that is to swim." So, he swam and swam, and swam, and churned a lump of butter and sat on it, and when the cover was lifted off, out he jumped.

"The Winner Never Quits—and the Quitter Never Wins!"

1245

If a melon clashes with a knife,
it is suicide and not heroism.

1246

Difficulty is an excuse which history never accepts.

1247

Discretion helps... always.

1248

The price of one year's
fast living is ten years of regret.

1249

Children are like wet cement.
Whatever falls on them makes an impression.

1250

When elephants fight, it's the grass that suffers.

1251

A rose given during life is better than
orchids on the grave.

1252

A good deed is one that brings a smile of joy
to the face of another.

1253

As host... offer fully.
As guest... take respectfully.

1254

Patients tend to heal in accordance with
their expectations.

The first step towards solving a problem is to begin.

1255

Concentrate all your thoughts upon
the work at hand. The sun's rays
do not burn until brought to a focus.

1256

Getting things done is important, but it is not as vital
as deciding what needs to be done.

1257

Destiny is not a matter of chance;
it is a matter of choice.

1258

Great things are not done by impulse but by
a series of small things brought together.

1259

Integrity is self rewarding.

1260

Why do we spend so much time and money
upgrading our possessions but not our thinking?

1261

Accounting is a teaching tool.

1262

Give credit, and lose your merchandise;
ask for payment, and gain an enemy.

1263

The only sure thing about luck is that it will change.

1264

The minor mistake is sometimes a
major improvement.

IF YOU
CAN DREAM IT,
YOU
CAN DO IT.
—Walt Disney

1265

It is all too easy to let yesterday's mistakes ruin today.
Train your mind to learn from your successes.

1266

The tide always comes back. Don't ever accept defeat.

1267

Common sense is very uncommon.

1268

Common sense is in spite of, not the result of,
education.

1269

Nothing great was ever achieved without enthusiasm.

1270

Good to forgive; best to forget.

1271

A gentleman is a man who can disagree
without being disagreeable.

1272

The only cure for grief is action.

1273

Honour lies in honest toil.

1274

Imagination is more important than knowledge.

1275

Men learn while they teach.

ON THINKING BIG...

Nikita S. Khrushchev went to his tailor with a bolt of expensive cloth especially woven for him. He asked the tailor to make up a three piece suit. After measuring the portly, vodka-guzzling red czar, the tailor said he would not have enough cloth for a vest. Khrushchev grumpily decided against ordering the suit and took the cloth with him on a visit to Belgrade. There he tried a Yugoslav tailor who measured him and found he could make a stylish suit including a vest. Khrushchev, puzzled, asked why the Russian tailor couldn't cut the cloth to make a vest. "In Moscow you are a bigger man than you are here," the Belgrade tailor replied.

Similarly, we all think we are bigger than we are. In our own establishments, each of us is secure and powerful; only when we move out do we come to know about our worth.

1276

A little nonsense now and then is relished
by the wisest men.

1277

The foolish and the dead alone
never change their opinion.

1278

In quarrelling the truth is always lost.

1279

At times "knowing" is when a man can say
"I do not know."

1280

Fatigue is the best pillow.

1281

The matchstick is a transportable and pocketable fire.
Before it was invented, people laughed at the idea
just as they do if someone today suggests having an
airconditioner the size of a pen.

1282

Wise men learn more from defeat than
they do from victory.

1283

Friends tell you what you have to hear.
Others will tell you what you want to hear.

1284

He allows his successes five minutes of crowing and
his failures a second's worth of bemoaning.

1285

Climbing steep hills requires a slow pace at first.

1286

The heart has no secret that our
conduct does not reveal.

1287

What I consider one of the many blessings in my life,
you have so far missed: being poor.

1288

Making money is a slow process; losing it can happen
quickly enough to make your head spin.

1289

No one has ever been able to purchase such ultimate
treasures as a good family, sound health,
true friends, loyal employees,
true love, or true respect.

1290

Reading is thinking with another person's mind;
it forces you to stretch your own.

1291

Simply because of my reading, I have already lived
the equivalent of about ten lifetimes of experience.

1292

That man is the richest whose
pleasures are the cheapest.

1293

The greatest mark of a man's being flawless is that he
does not seek flaws in others.

The greatest undeveloped territory in the world
lies under your hat.

1294

Don't hire a master to paint you a masterpiece
and then assign a roomful of school boys
to suggest improvements.

1295

Conviction should prevail.
Compromises should be avoided.

1296

When you're off on a business trip or a vacation,
pretend you're a customer.
Telephone some part of your organisation and ask for
help. You'll run into some real horror shows.

1297

The junior men always sat at the foot and I sat at the
head, and then I learned that the light of conviction is
often in the eyes of the junior men. With a round
table, I was closer to them and less likely to miss it.

1298

Keep in mind that first impressions of a performance
are often wrong. There are slow starters who become
stars, and flashes in the pan who sputter out.

1299

The British created a civil-service
job in 1803 calling for a man to stand on the Cliffs of
Dover with a spyglass. He was supposed to ring
a bell if he saw Napoleon coming.
The job was abolished in 1945.

God has given us a golden pen and a golden tongue. We overuse our tongue. Many of us can tell the President of the U.S.A. how to manage his country, but cannot even manage ourselves! Let us learn to use our pen. It is possible if we develop good reading habits. I suggest you ensure that Ma Saraswati sits together with Ma Laxmi in your home and in your office.

1300

Managers tend to make their biggest mistakes in
things they've previously done best.

1301

What I give out, I get back. I give out only goodness
and, in turn, only goodness comes back to me.

1302

My wonderful thoughts create my wonderful world.
I choose my thoughts with care.

1303

Today I do a mental housecleaning,
making room for new, positive thoughts.

1304

I look within to find my treasures.

1305

I focus on positive thoughts because the thoughts I
think and the words I speak create my experiences.

1306

My joyful thoughts create my joyful world.

1307

My mind is a tool I can choose to use any way I wish.

1308

Forgiveness is a gift to myself. It is easy and
rewarding for me to forgive.

1309

All experiences are opportunities for me
to learn and grow.

Don't cry over spilt soup...

An old Chinese farmer was walking along the road with a stick across his shoulder. Hanging from the stick was a pot filled with soyabean soup. He stumbled and the jar fell off and broke into pieces. The old farmer kept going, unperturbed. A man rushed up and said excitedly, "Don't you know that your jar broke?" "Yes," the old farmer answered. "I know. I heard it fall. It's broken; the soup is gone — what can I do about it?"

1310

Whenever I have a problem, I know it comes from limiting my thought patterns. I effortlessly solve my problems by choosing positive thoughts.

1311

I am as successful as I make up my mind to be.

1312

I appreciate all that I do.
I am the most important person in my life.

1313

Today is the future I created yesterday.

1314

It is safe to be flexible enough to
see other viewpoints.

1315

Other people respect me because I respect myself.

1316

One who has a book is not alone.

1317

My prosperous thoughts create my prosperous world.
Prosperity is attracted to me.

1318

I hear— I forget; I see—I remember;
I do—I understand.

1319

Behind an able man there are
always other able men.

1320

We judge overselves by what we feel capable of doing,
while others judge us by what we have already done.

1321

Adversity introduces a man to himself.

1322

Never answer a letter while you are angry.

1323

Carelessness does more harm than a want of knowledge.

1324

The wife of a careless man is almost a widow.

1325

In business, events of importance are
the result of trivial causes.

1326

Among mortals second thoughts are wisest.

1327

Little boats should keep near the shore.

1328

There is no pillow so soft as a clear conscience.

1329

He is well paid who is well satisfied.

1330

The discovery of a new dish does more for human
happiness than the discovery of a new star.

1331

The more corrupt the state, the more laws.

**OLD AGE IS NOT THE NAME OF AN OLD BODY—
IT IS THE NAME OF AN OLD MIND.**

1332

If you want the time to pass quickly,
just give your note for 90 days.

1333

Even the lion has to defend himself against flies.

1334

There are two tragedies in life: one is not to get your
heart's desire: the other is to get it.

1335

A diplomat is a man who remembers
a lady's birthday but forgets her age.

1336

Disappointment is the nurse of wisdom.

1337

No one can disgrace us but ourselves.

1338

What loneliness is more lonely than distrust.

1339

The best carpenters make the fewest chips.

1340

None preaches better than the ant,
and it says nothing!

1341

Experience is the extract of suffering.

1342

Overcoming the enemy by power is half a victory;
overcoming the enemy by love is a complete victory.

Which came first, the chicken or the egg? I believe the chicken came first! The chicken gets busy, scratching and scratching and starts getting sufficient worms and starts laying the "golden eggs." You will never find a stressful chicken. They are always too busy!

1343

A farmer is always going to be rich next year.

1344

Fear always springs from ignorance.

1345

There was a wise man in the East whose
constant prayer was that he might see today
with the eyes of tomorrow.

1346

Gratitude is the heart's memory.
He who receives a good turn should never forget it;
he who does one should never remember it.

1347

I have learned to seek my happiness by limiting my
desires, rather than in attempting to satisfy them.

1348

The first test of a truly great man is his humility.

1349

He is not only idle who does nothing,
but he is idle who might be better employed.

1350

If the nose of Cleopatra had been
half-an-inch shorter, the world's
history would have been different. Right?

1351

I fear three newspapers more than a
hundred thousand bayonets.

Change your thoughts, and you change your world.

1352

In Chinese, the word 'crisis' is composed of
two characters. One represents danger
and the other represents opportunity.

1353

Strange how much you've got to know before
you know how little you know.

1354

Only in quiet waters things mirror themselves
undistorted. Only in a quiet mind can there
be adequate perception of the world.

1355

A lawyer starts life giving Rs. 500 worth
of law for Rs. 50, and ends up giving Rs. 50
worth for Rs. 5000!

1356

Throw a lucky man into the sea,
and he will come up with a fish in his mouth!

1357

The best way to escape from your
problem is to solve it.

1358

Send your noble blood to market
and see what it will bring.

1359

Long sentences in a short composition are like large
rooms in a little house.

We cannot direct the wind... But we can adjust our sails.

Never run yourself down. Believe in yourself, esteem yourself not with egotism but with humble, realistic self-confidence. Stop brooding over the past. Drop the postmortems. Live enthusiastically. Starting today make the best you can of it. Give it all you've got and you will find that to be plenty.

ISBN 81-900019-2-2
Pages: 326
Size: 8½"x5½".
Price: Rs. 176 (PB)
Order No. A1

ISBN 81-900019-4-9
Pages: 492
Size: 8½"x5½".
Price: Rs. 266 (PB)
Order No. A2

ISBN 81-900547-7-5
Pages: 103
Size: 8½"x5½".
Price: Rs. 76 (PB)
Order No. A3

ISBN 81-86773-16-9
Pages: 320
Size: 8¾" x 5¾".
Price: Rs. 176
Order No. A4

ISBN 81-86773-11-6
Pages: 328
Size: 8½"x5½".
Price: Rs. 176 (PB)
Order No. A5

ISBN 81-900019-8-1
Pages: 101
Size: 8½"x5½".
Price: Rs. 76 (PB)
Order No. A6

ISBN 81-900547-9-1
Pages: 97
Size: 8½"x5½".
Price: Rs. 76 (PB)
Order No. A7

ISBN 81-900547-4-0
Pages: 265
Size: 8½"x5½".
Price: Rs. 156 (PB)
Order No. A8

ISBN 81-900547-8-3
Pages: 148
Size: 8½"x5½".
Price: Rs. 116 (PB)
Order No. A9

ISBN 81-86773-01-0
Pages: 142
Size: 8½"x5½".
Price: Rs. 116 (PB)
Order No. A10

ISBN 81-86773-34-7
Pages: 144
Size: 8½"x5½".
Price: Rs. 96 (PB)
Order No. A11

ISBN 81-867733-32-0
Pages: 144
Size: 8½"x5½".
Price: Rs. 96 (PB)
Order No. A12

MANAGING SELF & FAMILY BOOKS

**SIMPLE WAYS TO MAKE
YOUR FAMILY HAPPY**

PROMOD BATRA
VIJAY BATRA
DIVYA ARORA

HAPPINESS
IS A JOURNEY, NOT A
DESTINATION.

ISBN 81-86773-21-5
Pages: 411
Size: 8¾"x5¾".
Price: Rs. 196 (PB)
Order No. F1

Management Thoughts for the family

PROMOD BATRA
VIJAY BATRA

ISBN 81-900019-5-7
Pages: 354
Size: 8½"x5½"
Price: Rs. 176 (PB)
Order No. F2

**Simple Ways to
KEEP YOUR WIFE
HAPPY**

PROMOD BATRA

ISBN 81-900019-7-3
Pages: 37
Size: 8½"x5½".
Price: Rs. 46 (PB)
Order No. F3

PROMOD BATRA

**SIMPLE WAYS TO MAKE
YOUR HUSBAND
FEEL GREAT**

ISBN 81-900547-6-7
Pages: 83
Size: 8½"x5½".
Price: Rs. 76 (PB)
Order No. F4

**SIMPLE WAYS TO MAKE
YOUR SON
GOOD FOR EVERYTHING**

PROMOD BATRA

ISBN 81-900547-3-2
Pages: 99
Size: 8½"x5½".
Price: Rs. 76 (PB)
Order No. F5

**SIMPLE WAYS TO MAKE YOUR
DAUGHTER
WORLDLY-WISE**

PROMOD BATRA

ISBN 81-900547-2-4
Pages: 91
Size: 8½"x5½".
Price: Rs. 76 (PB)
Order No. F6

**SIMPLE WAYS TO
LIVE PEACEFULLY WITH
YOUR IN-LAWS**

PROMOD BATRA
RAKHSHANDA JALIL

ISBN 81-86773-03-7
Pages: 87
Size: 8½"x5½".
Price: Rs. 76 (PB)
Order No. F7

**Simple Ways to Enjoy Your
Grand Children**

Promod Batra
Rakhshanda Jalil

ISBN 81-86773-05-3
Pages: 109
Size: 8½"x5½".
Price: Rs. 76 (PB)
Order No. F8

CORPORATE GIFT BOOKS

**Pearls of Wisdom for
THE FAMILY**

PROMOD BATRA
RAKHSHANDA JALIL

ISBN 81-86773-05-3
Pages: 120
Size 5½"x4"
Price: Rs 76 (PB)
Order No. C1

**Pearls of Wisdom for
HAPPY LIVING**

ISBN 81-86773-17-7
Pages: 89
Size 5½"x4"
Price: Rs 76 (PB)
Order No. C2

**Pearls of Wisdom for
MANAGERS**

PROMOD BATRA
RAKHSHANDA JALIL

ISBN 81-86773-04-5
Pages: 156
Size 5½"x4"
Price: Rs 96 (HB)
Order No. C3

**SIMPLIFY
YOUR
LIFE
TO BE HAPPY**

PROMOD BATRA
VIJAY BATRA

ISBN 81-86773-20-7
Pages: 125
Size 6x4½"
Price: Rs 76 (PB)
Order No. C4

MANAGEMENT BOOKS (HINDI TRANSLATION)

ISBN 81-86773-19-3
Pages: 261
Size: 8½"×5½".
Price: Rs. 156 (PB)
Order No. H1

ISBN 81-86773-10-X
Pages: 111
Size: 8½"×5½".
Price: Rs. 76 (PB)
Order No. H2

ISBN 81-86773-00-2
Pages: 105
Size: 8½"×5½".
Price: Rs. 76 (PB)
Order No. H3

ISBN 81-86773-01-0
Pages: 160
Size: 8½"×5½".
Price: Rs. 116 (PB)
Order No. H4

ISBN 81-86773-12-6
Pages: 37
Size: 8½"×5½".
Price: Rs. 46 (PB)
Order No. H5

ISBN 81-86773-16-5
Pages: 83
Size: 8½"×5½".
Price: Rs. 76 (PB)
Order No. H6

ISBN 81-86773-15-0
Pages: 91
Size: 8½"×5½".
Price: Rs. 76 (PB)
Order No. H7

ISBN 81-86773-14-2
Pages: 104
Size: 8½"×5½".
Price: Rs. 76 (PB)
Order No. H8

ISBN 81-86773-00-2
Pages: 105
Size: 8½"×5½".
Price: Rs. 76 (PB)
Order No. H9

MANAGEMENT SUCCESSORIES (THINKING TRIGGERS™)

ADDRESS BOOK

ISBN 81-900547-1-6
Size: 9¾"x7¾".
Price: Rs. 136
Order No. S1

TELEPHONE INDEX

ISBN 81-86773-09-8
Size: 9"x5¾".
Price: Rs. 116
Order No. S2

DESK PLANNER

ISBN 81-86773-02-9
Size: 8¾"x11¾".
Price: Rs. 196
Order No. S3

THINKING KITS

ISBN 81-86773-01-0
No. 15 (Also in Hindi)
Size: 5¾"x4½".
Price: Rs. 376
Order No. S4

MANAGEMENT THOUGHTS POSTERS

ISBN 81-86773-05-3
No. 36 Size: 11"x11".
Price: Rs. 360 for 36 posters.
(Also in Hindi)
Order No. S5

LARGE POSTERS

Six large posters
Size: 18"x27" Price: Rs. 300
Order No. S6

TRAINING SLIDES

ISBN 81-86773-07-X
Price: Rs. 1800 for 36 slides; (35 mm)
(Also in Hindi)
Order No. S7

WALL PLANNER

ISBN 81-86773-04-5
Leaves: 14 Size: 11"x22
Price: Rs. 196
Order No. S8

THINK CARDS

ISBN 81-86773-06-6
55 cards Size: 2¼"x3½,
Price: Rs. 66
Order No. S9